Canucks by the Sea

The Canadian Army in Eastbourne during the Second World War

by

Michael Ockenden

By the same author
Situational Dialogues
Talking Points
Small Talk
Around Town

Translation
Wasserkrieg
by
Helmuth Euler
Published as
The Dams Raid through the Lens
by
After the Battle

Eastbourne Local History Society
www.eastbournehistory.org.uk

©Michael Ockenden 2006

ISBN 0 9547647 1 4

Printed and bound by CPI Antony Rowe, Eastbourne

Contents

This book is dedicated with grateful thanks to the men of the Canadian Army who served in Eastbourne during the Second World War.

Foreword

The best sign of a well-written book is the fact that when you sit down and start to read it you do not want to stop. This is such a book, but it also has the advantage of providing factual information from the Second World War about sites in Eastbourne and the surrounding area that can be visited today. I am pleased to be able to add my name to those of previous holders of the Mayoralty and pay tribute publicly to the Canadians and their contribution to Eastbourne's history.

Michael Ockenden should be thanked profusely for his hard work and thorough research into that history and the effects of our Canuck friends' time in Eastbourne. The book brings alive that period and provides a fascinating insight into everyday life during a most challenging period of time.

It is important to remember that the Canadian soldiers were essentially volunteers, and here because they believed in what needed to be done to maintain and defend democratic freedom. This book is a fitting tribute to the many of them who made the supreme sacrifice as well as to the legacy that the Canadians left behind in our town.

It is appropriately written in one record, "This Battalion feels that they belong to Eastbourne and Eastbourne belongs to them."

Councillor Graham Marsden
Mayor of Eastbourne
3 April 2006

1
After you've gone

'Ghost Town by the Sea' – thus was the description of Eastbourne by its MP, Major Charles Taylor, in an article in *Illustrated* on 27 March 1943. There are no figures but the exodus had begun with the fall of France in June 1940 when the area suddenly acquired front-line status. It was not only the residents who left. There had long been a tradition of boarding schools in Eastbourne; a pre-war *Kelly's* lists some 50 private schools in and around the town. Most of these would leave – the majority never to return. On 20 June, Eastbourne College was evacuated to Radley College in Oxfordshire.[1]

A naval rating on guard outside Powell House in Grange Road. When the mining and torpedo school at Portsmouth, HMS Vernon, was devastated by bombing, a new location was found at Roedean School near Brighton. In 1942, another RN underwater weapons school, HMS Marlborough, took over Eastbourne College. The secret work necessitated a high degree of security resulting in the closure of Grange Road between Carlisle Road and Blackwater Road; the same applied to Old Wish Road between Carlisle Road and Grange Road.

On 10 July, restrictions were placed on people entering a 20-mile coastal belt – a death knell for most of the hotels and boarding houses that tried to struggle on. Large houses were shut up as owners left the invasion zone. However, as the war progressed, these abandoned buildings would find a new role as local government offices, training establishments and billets for military personnel.

The CBOE Treasurer's Department moved to Granville Crest in Bolsover Road. There was a large RN contingent (HMS Marlborough, 1942–46) at Eastbourne College; the RAF trained aircrew (No 1 Elementary Air Observer School, 1941–43) and later airmen (Equipment Training School) in the seafront hotels.[2] Some of the first army units in the area were the 8th and 9th Battalions of The Devonshire Regiment, who were assigned to a coastal defence role from May 1940 until the autumn of that year.[3]

However, of all the armed services it was undoubtedly the Canucks – the men of the Canadian army – who made the greatest impression on the townspeople, and between the summer of 1941 and the run-up to D-Day Eastbourne was 'home' to thousands of Canadian soldiers.[*]

---

[*] Less familiar than Yank & Kiwi, Canuck is an informal term for Canadian. *The Oxford Companion to the English Language* states that while it historically might have been considered derogatory, it is now accepted by most Canadians, and used by them, with pride. The origin is probably from an Indian word meaning someone who lives in a 'kanata', or village.

2
We're on our way

The Dominion declared war on 10 September 1939 and the Canadian 1st Division reached Britain shortly before Christmas.

By the late summer of 1940, the Canadian 2nd Division had also crossed the Atlantic. Most of the troops were based in the Home Counties with a large concentration in and around Aldershot. By the end of the war nearly half a million Canadian servicemen and women would have come to Britain.[4] The first large influx to our area came as part of a move by the 2nd Canadian Division at the beginning of July 1941. The Canadians took over the beach defences on the greater part of the coast of East Sussex, relieving the British 55th Division, which moved to Aldershot. This movement had been partly inspired by a desire to give a salutary change to the troops involved. Aldershot had

Famous recruiting poster – one of a series which helped swell the Dominion's small pre-war army. Image courtesy of the Library and Archives of Canada.

not been a popular station with Canadian officers and men – a change of scene seemed the best means of combating the boredom. Officers confirmed that the move had a good effect on the morale of the Division.[5]

The three Regiments of the 2nd Division in the Eastbourne area at this stage of the war were: 1st Battalion, The Black Watch (Royal Highland Regiment) of Canada [Black Watch], Le Régiment de Maisonneuve [Maisonneuves] and The Calgary

Highlanders [Calgaries] – all part of the 5th Canadian Infantry Brigade, whose HQ was at Crossways House in Upper Dicker.[6]

Security dictated that there would be no reference in local newspapers to the Canadian arrival, but the *Eastbourne Chronicle* published a cryptic letter from a resident on 12 July 1941. Pleading for better facilities for 'our visitors', the writer complains that they had been moved along by an attendant from deckchairs on the parade. Playing with the double meaning of the word 'front', the correspondent comments: 'These visitors have sacrificed so much to get to the front.'

The Canucks had arrived and were eager to get to the battlefront. However, during the First World War, there had also been a Canadian presence in the town, but these had mostly been men returning from the front. In 1917, the Canadians set up their own 16th General Hospital at All Saints in Darley Road and at St Luke's in Cliff Road. Staffed and equipped entirely by the Dominion, the hospital could take up to 700 cases.

During the epidemic of Spanish influenza at the end of the Great War, 70 young Canadian soldiers, from the Railway Construction Camps at Seaford, died from influenza in All Saints Hospital and were returned to Seaford for burial.[7]

3
This desirable residence

Fresh from barracks at Aldershot or long periods under canvas, Canadian troops could hardly believe their luck when they saw the standard of accommodation in Eastbourne. The Calgaries moved into the town in December 1941. The War Diary indicates that they were initially allocated Battle Positions at Hailsham but as there were practically no billeting facilities, a decision was taken to move into Eastbourne, leaving just one platoon and some transport in the market town. This must have proved popular because the men found themselves in a prime residential district – in and around Prideaux Road. Many of the houses in this and adjoining roads had been designed to an exceptionally high standard by Eastbourne's premier architect of the inter-war years, Peter Stonham.

Wayside, at the junction of Mill and Prideaux Roads, was used as a Canadian Officers' Mess and is typical of the large houses taken over by the army in the Upperton area.

The War Diary for 15 December 1941 notes: 'Billets in Eastbourne are very satisfactory, mostly new houses now vacated. Engineers are installing blackout and carrying out electrical repairs.' At Action Stations, troops would move to Hailsham and occupy Battle Positions. The RHQ was at Prideaux Place, and the RHQ Officers' Mess at Wayside in Mill Road. Satisfaction is reaffirmed later in the month: 'The new billets are like palaces compared with some we have known. All are practically new houses that have been evacuated earlier in the war. There are hardwood floors and the houses have every modern convenience.'

In fact, officers of the Calgaries were concerned that life might have become too easy: 'Many of our men have married and live only till they see their wives again, as a great number of them have brought their wives to Eastbourne and have "sleeping-out" passes. Others, less fortunate in the matrimonial line, just simply hang around.'[8] However, the spell of comfortable living was over for the Regiment by the spring. On 1 May 1942, the Diary gives their location as Highlands Wood to the west of Hailsham.

With regard to the level of occupancy, the Regimental Association of The Edmonton Regiment [Edmontons] states that when they were in Upperton in 1942, some houses accommodated 15 men and others 50. It should be borne in mind that a regiment consisted of some 800 men. Whereas regimental papers usually provide key locations – headquarters, messes, aid posts etc – the whereabouts of individual billets are seldom given.

Although Prideaux Road was the central line, buildings were occupied across a wide area. For the Upperton sector alone, the author has come across references to the following roads: Arundel, Ashburnham, Carew, Commercial, Enys, Le Brun, Lewes and Upper Avenue. However, it is unlikely that the full extent of occupation can now be ascertained. Although owners were compensated, such records were held at the National Archives in the Defence Lands Branch of MoD, but have since been destroyed.

Although there were vacant houses, accommodation was hard to find. The Black Watch received orders to move from Willingdon to Meads, and on 5 December 1941 the Diary records: 'During both morning and afternoon, recce's of possible new billets were made. Despite the large number of buildings which should be available for occupancy because of civilian evacuation, it is not always easy to find billets which satisfy all our requirements. Many of the best billets in the western edge of the town have already been taken by the 31st Tank Brigade [a British formation] on their arrival in October.' However, by the time of the move from Willingdon to Meads on 18 December 1941, they had procured a fine house for their Regimental Headquarters – St Rita's in Paradise Drive.

St Rita's was RHQ of the Black Watch from 19 Dec 41-19 Feb 42. No 89 Battery, 1 Canadian LAA had its HQ here on 3 April 1943 when the town was raided. One target was HMS Marlborough at Eastbourne College, where staff had heard rumours (attributed to Lord Haw Haw) of a raid. German broadcasts had said nothing, but the Diary of the LAA unit quotes intelligence reports of an expected raid that weekend. This must have been the information which had filtered through to HMS Marlborough.

If St Rita's became untenable in the event of an invasion, the RHQ would withdraw to a Battle HQ in Paradise Wood near the reservoir, which was then unused and open to the elements: 'The Battle HQ offers good concealment and good intercommunication with A, B and D Companies.'

The Officers' Mess was Cloona, 38 Carlisle Road, at the corner of Link Road and near to RHQ. The officers were impressed: 'This is no doubt the most comfortable abode we have had in England – compared with last winter, when we practically lived on the roads during tactical schemes and MT [Motor Transport] moves, we're all living in the lap of luxury.' On the evening of 25 December 1941, the officers at Cloona sat down to a meal which was followed by a rather special pudding: 'H M Queen Elizabeth, our Colonel-in-Chief, had sent us enough Xmas Pudding for the entire Battalion, which was much appreciated. Altogether this is a pleasant Xmas in pleasant surroundings.'

The problem of accommodation persisted into the New Year. On 26 January 1942, the Black Watch reiterates: 'There are not enough empty buildings to house the entire unit and we may have to requisition occupied houses, which is proving to be a most unpopular move.' In the event, this was not required. Already on 19 January the Diary reports a suggestion that another move was afoot: 'It seems we shall be obliged to move the Battalion [back] to Willingdon. We shan't like giving up our comfortable billets.'

One month later, most of the Regiment had returned to Willingdon, its RHQ at Malaya House in Park Lane: 'Providing the wise-crackers with ample opportunity for comment on the Army's interpretation of a mobile force!' However, the change was due to operational requirements: 'The return is a nuisance but, if our operational role is to exclude the defence of the foredown behind Beachy Head, it is unwise to think of leaving any parts of the Battalion down in Eastbourne old town.' The diarist had clearly not been in Eastbourne long enough to distinguish between Old Town and Meads.

Bishop Carey in Gaudick Road was known as Westbrook until taken over by Ascham School after the war. This and Sunnymead next door were occupied by Canadian LAA units. Westbrook had been the home of Lady Minoru Foley, an eccentric, and leading light in the social and charity scene during the 1930s. Her son, Lord Adrian Foley, was a talented pianist. In 1940, at the age of 17, he wrote a song which Noel Gay, the music publisher, predicted would be the song of the war. Alas it was never to attain such heights.

There are few references to Canadian forces being quartered in Eastbourne's hotels, many of which had been taken over by the RAF. However, it is known from a Location Statement that 73rd Field Battery of The 5th Field Regiment RCA [5 Fd Regt] was at the Glendower Hotel in Burlington Place in February 1942.*

The Lansdowne Hotel had been cleared of all furniture in September 1940 to provide quarters for personnel of 342 Coastal Battery RA, who manned the two naval guns at the Wish Tower. Between 4 March and 19 April 1942, the Lansdowne was occupied by an element of the 4th Canadian Infantry Brigade – A Company of The Royal Regiment of Canada. However, after a few weeks of comfort at this seafront hotel, the Regiment moved under canvas at Hellingly. In August 1942, they would take part in 'Operation Jubilee', the raid against Dieppe.

---

* Also in February 1942, the 5th Field Battery of the same regiment moved from Glynleigh to St Andrew's School in Meads. The Diary notes: 'It is the first time in some months that 5 Bty HQ and the two troops have been accommodated under one roof. The building was formerly used for a boys school and will sleep roughly 250 men.' The Diary of Le Régiment de Maisonneuve notes the gun sites of 5 Fd Regt's 25-pounders as follows: 5 Bty, A Trp (MR 581015 – Beehive Plantation), B Trp (MR 583082 – by B 2104 near Hailsham Cemetery), OP (MR 577022 – path behind Butts Brow); 28 Bty, C Trp (MR 582087 – by A 295 south of Hailsham), D Trp (MR 584087 – by A 295 south of Hailsham), OP Stone Cross Windmill; 73 Bty, E Trp (MR 618044 – by Peelings Lane), F Trp (MR 585085 – by B 2104 near Hailsham Cemetery), OP (MR 631049 – Mill Hill). For information about wartime map references see page 43.

4
Collateral damage

Ratton Manor at Willingdon had been the home of the Freeman-Thomas family. As Lord Willingdon, Freeman Freeman-Thomas was Governor General of Canada from 1926 to 1931 and Viceroy of India from 1931 to 1936. He had the mansion rebuilt in 1899 following a fire in December 1891.[9] The Manor burnt down again in December 1940; it is rumoured that the blaze occurred when Canadian soldiers were billeted there.

Ratton Manor, the former home of Lord Willingdon. When the house burnt down in 1940, it was rumoured that Canadians had been in occupation. However, no evidence has been found in official records.

The late W J Vine writes in *Old Willingdon*: 'It was during the [Canadian] occupation that Ratton, for the second time in its history, was completely gutted by fire, this time never to rise from its ashes.' The author attended a meeting of Eastbourne Local History Society in November 1976 when Mr Vine mentioned the fire during a talk about Ratton, adding that prisoners of war had also been kept on the top floor. Unfortunately, Mr Vine had no direct knowledge of the fire or the POWs as he had been away in the forces at the time. However, during research for this book, the author interviewed Mrs Parris of Wish Hill, who recalled a rumour that Canadian soldiers who had been confined to barracks had been roasting a pig in an attic fireplace when the fire broke out!

The author has examined the War Diaries of many units, but failed to find any mention of the fire. The only reference discovered thus far to Canadians in Eastbourne during December 1940 stems from the War Diary of the Royal Montreal Regiment [RMR], which states that their B Company was sent to Eastbourne from Sutton for two weeks on 23 November to work with a British regiment, The Buffs. On 7 December they returned to Sutton: 'Feeling rather depressed that they had not experienced any action during their sojourn.' Over Christmas, C Company of the RMR was in Eastbourne from 21 December 1940 to 4 January 1941. Unfortunately there is no record of where they were located, but

anything as serious as a fire would have been logged. Reports in local papers were subject to censorship and provide no clue to the origin of the blaze. The *Eastbourne Chronicle* says only that the Manor had been used until earlier in the year by Southdown College; the cause of the outbreak was unknown but was not due to enemy action. No further information is given in other local newspapers.

The story of Canadian involvement is so widely held that it seems hardly conceivable it could be untrue. Yet in wartime, false rumours spread fast. Most people believed that 'Lord Haw Haw' had said in broadcasts that the town hall clock in Darlington was ten minutes fast and that he had predicted air raids. However, BBC Written Archives comment: 'We are often asked to investigate rumours that 'Lord Haw-Haw' had predicted the bombing of some specific target but this has never proved to be the case.' As far as the fire at Ratton is concerned, until further evidence reveals otherwise, the circumstances remain unclear.

The above picture showing the Black Watch in what must be the ruins of Ratton Manor is courtesy of the Canadian Department of National Defence and was taken in March 1942. The Regiment had also been in the area in 1941, when Ratton Manor was earmarked as their Battalion Headquarters in the event of an invasion.

The Manor is quoted by the Black Watch on 25 July 1941: 'It should be mentioned that our BHQ in the event of an invasion will be Ratton House [sic], formerly the home of Lord Willingdon, who was Governor General of Canada. Above Ratton House, on the fringe of the Downs is our observation post from where one gets a wonderful view of Eastbourne.' Pictures taken by an army photographer in 1942 show troops training in woodland and assaulting a large house – almost certainly Ratton Manor.

Whether or not the fire had occurred while Canadians were present, accommodation was at a premium and officers did their best to ensure that billets were respected. Apart from anything else, this helped allay the fears of those owners who were disinclined to rent their properties to the War Department. Furniture and carpets were removed before houses were handed over and staircase nosings were protected from the wear and tear of boots by battens fixed to each tread. Deductions were levied against pay to cover damage – as soldiers of the Black Watch discovered to their cost. On 15 November 1941 the Diary notes:

'Another one shilling assessment was made against the men's pay on this pay-day as a result of barrack damages and deficiencies from previous billets. It was a bitter shock to the troops to find that the threat of their pay being taxed to pay for barrack charges should actually be put into effect. They had held the comfortable belief that this threat was merely a bluff.'

Standing Orders issued to the Edmontons in August 1942 include the following note about damage.

Barrack Damages

1. Company Commanders will carry out a monthly check of all billets in order to reduce barrack damages.

2. In all cases where barrack damages occur, a list of all personnel occupying such billets will be made and forwarded to this HQ every month.

3. All personnel occupying billets where barrack damages occur will be assessed the full value of damage.

Despite the gravity of the wartime situation, the military were certainly not given free rein. In the autumn of 1942, the Edmontons were ordered to move an assault course from the playing field of Lynchmere [corner of Carew and Ashburnham Roads] due to: 'Objections from the matrons of the school, which is now closed'. A new location was found on the football pitch of the Grange, the former school in St Anne's Road where The Quadrant now stands: 'This field serves as a parade ground for the Battalion for all Battalion parades, and it is to be hoped we will be left in peace.'

Bombed houses in the Bourne Street area were used for training in house-to-house fighting by various units, including No 10 Inter-Allied Commando, Canadian infantry regiments and the Home Guard. Every attempt was made to create a realistic battle situation. The above picture from the Eastbourne Chronicle of 6 November 1943 includes three men in German uniforms at the Home Guard Battle Training School. On at least one occasion the owner of a wrecked house sought compensation!

Fortunately, the new arrangements for the assault course did indeed prove satisfactory. This is revealed by the War Diary of the Edmontons on 23 December 1942: 'Erected on the playing field of the Grange School is a 30-foot tower and hanging down one side is a 16-foot scaling net. This is to train the troops in scrambling up the side of a ship from a landing craft, and it's most interesting to see just how well the men make the ascent.'

At about the same time, the Diary complains: 'Street fighting can no longer be carried out in the bombed area of Eastbourne [Bourne Street] and therefore it is necessary to improvise, which naturally does not bring realism into the training. It seems the bombed houses, which are in a very derelict state, are still of some value, hence the Army has received orders to discontinue their use for street and village fighting.' However, this decision was later reversed as indicated by a report in the *Eastbourne Chronicle* which describes a Home Guard exercise in November 1943 at 'Hell Fire Corner' – the name given to Bourne Street after the bombing which had caused such destruction earlier in the war. Indeed, the Canadians continued at the Eastbourne Street Fighting School until at least 29 March 1944 when it was the venue for a demonstration by The Lake Superior Regiment (Motor).[10]

Further concern is noted in August 1943 when a Standing Order of The 23rd Field Regiment (SP) RCA [23 Fd Regt] states:

> *'The gardens of Regimental HQ, The Moorings,* [St John's Road] *are out of bounds to all ranks. The gardens forming part of the grounds of billets are out of bounds. Any fruit or vegetables grown under the Army Agricultural Scheme will neither be purchased nor purloined. Civilian gardeners will report infringements. No writing or marking of any kind on doors, walls or any part of billets. No nails or screws to be used. Notices are to be fixed by adhesives.'*

Yet this Standing Order was ignored as far as the boundary wall of the Moorings is concerned. The author's paper-round in the 1950s included the elegant Edwardian property which once occupied the site of the present block. Trees in the garden of this house in St John's Road provided shelter, and one morning the names of Canadian states and towns were spotted in the rain-

soaked wall. One name had been etched deeper than the others –
'Murray Bronson, Pictou, Nova Scotia'.

**Sheltering from the rain on his paper round in the 1950s, the author
spotted a name in the boundary wall of the Moorings in St John's Road.
The former soldier was traced to Novia Scotia – detective work which
sparked an interest in the Canadian Army in Eastbourne.**

A request for information to the local newspaper in Pictou
brought a reply from a surprised Murray Bronson, who had no
recollection of carving his name, but did have fond memories of
his stay in Eastbourne with 23 Fd Regt. The etched names and a
deep 'V' for Victory are now badly weathered, but still legible in
the brickwork.

There was considerable local resentment at the destruction of Belle Tout lighthouse by Canadian artillery fire in 1943. The story of the firing range at Birling Gap is covered in Chapter 22.

5
Caterpillar tracks

Meads residents often talk of the 'Canadian tanks' which were parked along Milnthorpe Road and Upper Dukes Drive. These belonged to The 23rd Field Regiment (SP) RCA of the Canadian 4th Armoured Division – the unit best remembered by those who lived in this part of town during the war.

A Sexton self-propelled gun as used by three Canadian artillery regiments overseas – 8th Field, 19th Field and 23rd Field. The 8th and 19th were in Eastbourne briefly; the 23rd for eight months. The Sextons caused considerable damage to pavements and roads in Meads.

Although they looked like tanks, they were mainly Sexton self-propelled 25-pounder guns. Weighing some 25 tons, the Sexton was a formidable machine, 20 feet long and towering eight feet above the ground. It had been developed from the Canadian Ram tank, which never saw active service under this name. The 23 Fd Regt was also equipped with Forward Observation Tanks (Rams), which carried additional radio equipment and plotting tables so that fire from their Sextons could be directed. However, the Forward Observation Tanks carried no shells, and the 'gun' was a piece of four-inch pipe welded to the turret to deceive the enemy: such a mobile command post would be a prime target. Yet a keen observer might have spotted extra radio aerials and reels of field-telephone cable on the rear engine decking.

On 8 August 1943, the gunners arrived from a reception camp at Chobham Common. The Regimental History states:

> *'Eastbourne turned out to be a beautiful seaside city, nestling behind the promontory of Beachy Head. Great hotels lined the parade which ran for several miles along the seafront. A large part of the population had been evacuated and it was into their homes in the western end of the city known as 'Meads Village' that the 23rd moved.*[11]

The Regiment consisted of the HQ Battery and three separate gun batteries – the 31st, the 36th and the 83rd, all of which had been raised in Ontario.[12] By piecing together information from former members of the Regiment, referring to the official history and consulting the War Diary, it has been possible to establish the approximate disposition of the various elements.

The 31st Battery, with A and B Troops, was centred on Dalton, Derwent and Milnthorpe Roads. Its Sextons were parked in Milnthorpe Road and under camouflage nets in the playing field in Darley Road by All Saints Hospital. Interviewed at her Milnthorpe Road home, where she had lived all her life, the late Babs Clements [née Hunter] recalled:

> *'They had armed guards at each end of Milnthorpe Road. Number 9 used to be the Sergeants' Mess and I went across for a party one night. They kept their ammunition in the garage. The bottom of Chesterfield Road was barricaded*

with pebbles. Kepplestone Flats on the seafront were barricaded, too. They had only just been finished, the roof only just having gone on. There were a couple of people living in them, but the rest of the building was rented to Canadian officers and their wives.'

The War Diary records that the Officers' Mess of the 31st Battery moved to the Ridge in Bolsover Road on 30 December 1943, but it is not known where it had been located prior to this.

Bob Eakin of the 36th Battery confirmed that the gunners of D Troop were billeted at 20 Edensor Road, with C Troop two doors up; their kitchen was next door but one, down the road. The Battery HQ was in Upper Dukes Drive, where their guns and other vehicles were parked. The officers and sergeants shared a mess at Tudor Croft in Baslow Road; the officers were accommodated on the lower floors and the sergeants in the eaves.

In September 1990, three former soldiers of the 36th Battery, 23 Fd Regt paid a return visit to Edensor Road in Meads, where they had been billeted from August 1943 to March 1944. From left to right – Bill Cockburn, Bill Corbett and Herb Danter.

Larry Holleran of the 83rd Battery remembers that he was billeted with E Troop at the corner of Edensor Road, and that a Lord and Lady Parker lived next door. [The 1940 *Kelly's* gives Sir Geo Lambert KCSI at Priors Down, 16 Edensor Road.] F Troop was further up the road and there was a tank barricade just round the corner. Their Battery HQ was at Holywell Priory with its large front garden. This property was demolished in the 1950s and the site redeveloped to create the present Holywell Close.* The location was popular because the Pilot was accessible even when men were confined to the barracks area!

Holywell Priory in Edwardian times. The house stood on the site of the present Holywell Close and was owned by the eccentric Countess de Noailles from 1868 until her death in 1908. The Countess kept a cow on the ground floor with holes to the master bedroom above because she believed the smell to be healthy. She left Eastbourne for Hyères in France in 1889, never to return. She maintained the house, which was used for holidays by her relations until its sale in 1911. The kitchen was haunted but Canadian troops at the Priory reported no ghostly sightings.

---

*The boundary wall onto Meads Street has four embrasures, but it is not known whether they were made by the Canadians or the Home Guard. These are probably the last ones remaining in the town.

The Sergeants' Mess of the 83rd was at Meads End, now part of St Bede's School. Some of their vehicles were also parked in Cliff Road. Houses in Cliff Road and Dukes Drive were taken over by the army at other times during the war.

This picture from *Eastbourne 1939-1945* was taken before D-Day and shows artillerymen in Cliff Road with a Sherman of the Guards Armoured Division, which moved into the Brighton-Eastbourne area in April 1944. Interestingly, this tank of The 153rd (Leicestershire Yeomanry) Field Regiment, RA (TA) was a Forward Observation Tank which would later work with British Sextons in Normandy. Its gun would have been a dummy. At the rear is part of the deep-wading gear fitted to tanks which came ashore from landing craft. The words 'West Norfolk' probably relate to the Battery Commander's home, or even to that of the driver.

Glenn Murphy was Regimental Quartermaster and arrived with the advance party. He recalls that the RHQ billets finally settled behind the Grand Hotel. Local people report seeing Canadian troops on the open ground behind 1–39 Jevington Gardens, and so the HQ may well have been on that side. Other ranks were in this area, but the RHQ Officers' Mess was at Bydown, the large house which stood on the site of today's 5 Chesterfield Road.

Officers of 23 Fd Regt in the rear garden of Bydown in Chesterfield Road. The house was distinctive for the Virginia creeper which covered its walls front and back. Note the sticky tape on the windows to limit injury from flying glass. The CO, Lieutenant Colonel K N Lander, has a moustache and stands in the centre foreground. On the extreme left is Major Hogarth, who assumed command when Lander was injured in Normandy. In the second row, Captain Glenn Murphy, the Regimental Quartermaster, is second from the right; his brother, Captain Rodger Murphy, stands behind Major Hogarth.

Glenn's brother, Rodger, was Technical Adjutant in the HQ Battery and had graduated from the technical school of General Motors. This, together with experience in the family motor firm, made him the ideal man to oversee the mechanical work on the vehicles. It was a heavy responsibility for in addition to 24 Sextons, the Regiment was also equipped with 12 Forward Observation Tanks, 12 Troop Leader Tanks, which were the same as the Forward Observation Tanks, numerous half-track vehicles, Bren Carriers, Jeeps, trucks and motor cycles.

The Diary reveals a certain amount of chopping and changing before the accommodation was sorted out. Highmead in Buxton Road was initially the RHQ, but this soon moved to 9 Milnthorpe

Road, and then to the Moorings in St John's Road. The top floor of the latter was also used by F Troop of the 4th (Armoured) Divisional Signals. The Light Aid Detachment (No. 104 Light Aid Detachment (Type D), RCOC) was eventually transferred to 9 Milnthorpe Road. Highmead became a billet for other ranks. Crosby Lodge, subsequently the residence of the headmaster of Ascham, and now in Gaudick Close, was where men could find the Educational Corporal, who would advise them on courses they could attend at universities when on leave.

Glendale Mackay with a 1929 Buick in front of Bydown, where he was chauffeur to the Megaw family. He was killed when a bomb fell on Meads Street on 7 March 1943. During the same raid another bomb destroyed the former St Augustine's School in Milnthorpe Road, which was then a billet for the Canadian 2 Fd Regt. By September 1943, Bydown had become an Officers' Mess for 23 Fd Regt.

Although the troops were accommodated in fine houses, there were no regular hot baths; in the mornings, men in the immediate area also used lavatories and basins in the public toilets on the slope to the Holywell Tea Chalet. However, there was always the Devonshire Baths – a location mentioned by many units. The official history of 23 Fd Regt states: 'A weekly feature for each troop was a bath and swim parade at the Devonshire Baths wearing a moth-eaten Gay Nineties bathing suit which cost a few pence.'

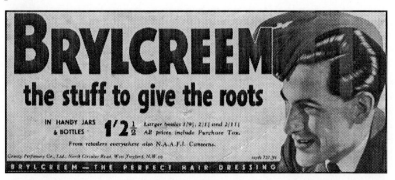

BRYLCREEM

the stuff to give the roots

IN HANDY JARS & BOTTLES · **1′2½** · *Larger bottles 1/9½, 2/1½ and 2/11½ All prices include Purchase Tax.*

From retailers everywhere also N.A.A.F.I. Canteens.

County Perfumery Co., Ltd., North Circular Road, West Twyford, N.W.10

BRYLCREEM — THE PERFECT HAIR DRESSING

The RAF were known as 'Brylcreem Boys' and large numbers of airmen were trained at former schools and seafront hotels. There were compulsory bath and swim parades at the Devonshire Baths in Carlisle Road for all servicemen – the attendants joked that they had to skim the Brylcreem off the surface after the RAF had been in!

Inevitably the mighty Sextons took their toll of the roads and brick pavements of Meads. The latter suffered because vehicles had to be left partly on the pavement and partly on the road. Babs Clements remembered:

'At times, there were 15 tanks on the pavements in Milnthorpe Road. They made a dreadful mess. The field at the side of All Saints used to be called Aldro Field because it belonged to the school. They parked their tanks in there as well, and when they came out they were so smothered in mud that the whole of Milnthorpe Road was like a muddy field; they had to open the fire hydrants to wash down the road. After the war, the Council lifted all the decent bricks from this side to re-lay the pavement on the other side, but this side [even numbers] *was patched up with any old stuff.'*

This method of repair was effected elsewhere in Meads, and also in Upperton. It is unclear when repairs were carried out, but it is interesting that brick pavements can also be seen along one side only of other roads where troops were based: Dalton, Darley, Derwent, Edensor, Rowsley, St Anne's and Selwyn Roads. By the autumn, the Council was concerned. The following is recorded in the War Diary on 2 October 1943: 'The Borough Engineer interviewed us regarding the damage to roads caused by Sextons. There is to be a recce of our routes to training areas so that the minimum of damage is caused.'

Highmead in Buxton Road was one of the houses in Meads taken over by the Canadians. It was initially the RHQ of 23 Fd Regt, but later became accommodation for other ranks and a venue for film shows.

Bob Eakin recalled that once or twice their Sextons crashed through the walls of St Andrew's School below Edensor Road. They soon learned that they could not barge through woodland as they had done in Canada. For knocking down a tree by the wall of St Andrew's they were fined £20. It was one of the tasks of Glenn and Rodger Murphy to liaise with the CBOE and property owners over compensation for damage.

Glenn Murphy – Then and Now
The above wartime shot of Rodger (left) and Glenn Murphy (right) dates from 1944 and shows the brothers sitting on what may be the barrel of a Sexton in Belgium or Holland. Rodger died in 1981, but Glenn is a hale and hearty 89-year-old. To the right, he proudly wears his campaign medals and RCA blazer before a veterans' parade at St Catherines, Ontario in April 2005. He and his wife, Verna, were married in 1941.

The Regiment left Eastbourne for Pippingford Park in Ashdown Forest, near Nutley, on 17 March 1944.[13] Their action in Normandy and North-western Europe is summarised in Chapter 23.

6
Something about a soldier

At the end of the Regiment's first visit, the Diary of the Black Watch notes on 11 August 1941: 'People in Eastbourne seem genuinely sorry to see us go. We were beginning to feel very much at home and there's no doubt that the stay here has been the most pleasant time we've been having in England, as yet.'

Relations between Canadians and locals were generally good. This is confirmed time and again from both sides of the Atlantic. The Diary notes on 20 July 1942: 'We were informed that we would relieve the 3rd Division in Eastbourne on 25 July 1942. This is very good news as this Battalion feels that they belong to Eastbourne and Eastbourne belongs to them. Since our first visit there, many men have married Eastbourne girls.' On 26 July, the Diary notes: 'The men took good advantage of the full day to spend with their girls and friends in Eastbourne.' And on 30 July: 'The troops were paid this morning so there will probably be a good time in the old town tonight.' At the end of the detachment the Diary states: 'Everyone was very sorry our stay in Eastbourne was at an end; it was wonderful having billets again with hot and cold running water, and being able to go up and down stairs and not just in and out of a tent flap. It was a very delightful week.'*

In any event, the Black Watch deserved their week of Rest and Recreation; the following month, three of their platoons would take part in 'Operation Jubilee', the raid against Dieppe. Virtually every man who landed became a prisoner and one officer was killed.[14]

The Eastbourne girls who married men of the Black Watch formed part of over 40,000 wives and nearly 20,000 children who

---

* The Regiment had also been in the area from 3 Jul-12 Aug 1941 (Willingdon); from 9 Oct-18 Dec 1941 (Willingdon); from 19 Dec 1941-19 Feb 1942 (Meads); from 20 Feb-15 May 1942 (Willingdon).

went to the Dominion; these exceeded even those who travelled to the USA – the latter 34,000 GI Brides and 14,000 children.[15]

Informally known as 'Quacks', three companies of the CWAC served at CMHQ in London, and a fourth at Reinforcement Unit HQ in Aldershot. The poster, 'Shoulder to Shoulder', is courtesy and copyright the Canadian War Museum © (CWM).

A few of the marriages included Canadian Women's Army Corps [CWAC] personnel and those between a Canadian and a partner who was not British – but the vast majority involved Canadian servicemen and British women.[16] All the dependants received free passage to their new homes. This was the first time in history that any government had provided any form of home-to-home transportation for the dependants of its armed services.[17] Although a few women and children managed to get across as early as 1942, most had to wait until after the war – servicemen obviously had priority. It was an immense logistical task given the non-existence of commercial air services and the loss of shipping during the war. The arrival of the war brides must have marked the largest single wave of immigration since the Great Depression.

It fell to the Army to organise transport for dependants – not only for its soldiers, but also for the Dominion's sailors and airmen as well. An organisation called the Canadian Wives Bureau was set up above the Galleries Lafayette in Regents

Street.* Pre-war transatlantic liners such as the Queens and the Ile de France were converted from the trooping role which they had played during the war. Two hundred and fifty personnel of the Army Conducting Staff escorted dependants on the voyage. These consisted of Royal Canadian Army Service Corps, doctors, nursing sisters and Voluntary Aid Detachments (VADs), in which the Red Cross was a major player.[18] However, such was the pressure on transportation that some dependants had to wait until 1947 before joining their husbands – the last escorted passage was that of the SS Aquitania in January 1947.[19]

'Now that the war's over, we'll be leaving for Uncle Herbie's big ranch in Toronto.' **Some soldiers exaggerated their lifestyle in Canada. Bing Coughlin's 'Herbie' appeared in *Maple Leaf*, the Canadian Army's publication. The above cartoon appears courtesy of the Canadian Forces.**

According to the *Eastbourne Gazette* of 23 January 1946, some 150 Eastbourne girls had married Canadians. Around 100 were present at the inaugural meeting of the town's Canadian Wives Group. The Mayor, Alderman E C Martin, said he was glad that so many local girls had married the men who had come to Britain in our darkest hour. A representative of the Canadian Wives Bureau attended the meeting at Eastbourne Town Hall, where he revealed: 'Across the country even now

---

*With the German surrender, most Canadian servicemen in Germany were relocated to Holland. Later 1,886 Dutch war brides would also travel to Canada assisted by a branch of the Canadian Wives Bureau in The Hague.

Canadians are marrying British women at the rate of 1,000 per month.'

But what a step into the unknown it must have been for any girl with no experience of foreign travel, save perhaps a day-trip to Boulogne from Eastbourne Pier. A tearful farewell to friends and family at Southampton or Liverpool would often be followed by a rough crossing and, in many cases, the responsibility of looking after a child while trying to fight off seasickness. The ship would dock at Pier 21 in Halifax, Nova Scotia (now a historical site), and hopefully her husband and his family would be there to greet her. But would he have changed? How would she settle in and what kind of welcome could be expected from her in-laws? In many cases, the joys of life in the wide-open spaces would have been exaggerated; loneliness and homesickness would follow. In the 1940s, there were no budget airlines, no e-mail and no direct phone calls home.*

One Eastbourne girl, Mary Alkenbrack (née Martin), faced additional difficulties. The Canadian *Globe and Mail* of 16 April 1946 describes her as 'Canada's first blind war bride.' She saw her husband, George, then a Sergeant in The Hastings and Prince Edward Regiment [HPER], for only 11 days before he left England for the Continent. However, by the time he returned, she had been blinded by a V-1. The newspaper states that she went for a walk in 'Manor House Park' [presumably Manor Gardens] one bright summer's day. Suddenly the sirens screamed and everyone dived for cover as a V-1 exploded overhead. The Canadian report does not give a date, but it was probably 1 August 1944, when a V-1 was hit in the air above Old Town.

Mary Alkenbrack said: 'The flash and explosion was terrific – the whole back of my eyes seemed to crack from the force of it.' On her way home, everything went misty and as the days passed the world grew dimmer. She had three operations but became

*Accounts of the experiences of war brides can be found at www.canadianwarbrides.com

almost totally blind. She and her fiancé married when he had leave in July 1945. The *Globe and Mail* states that Mary hoped to regain her sight; she talked of the future in the little house which her husband had built while he awaited her arrival from England.

In May 1946, the tone remains upbeat – the Canadian National Institute for the Blind had sent an electric stove because of the difficulties she had experienced with a wood-burning range. A retired eye specialist had written from Florida offering to come to Canada to operate: 'Tell Mary to cheer up – she shall see.' However, less than a year later, the *Hamilton Spectator* reports that Mary had found the adjustment too difficult and would be returning with her Canadian husband to England early in February.

Thayendanegea, ancestor of William Brant – a Canadian married to an Eastbourne girl who was killed by a V-1. Brant was a sniper, forever haunted by the memory of his first victim – a German soldier sitting with a book.

Coincidentally, the lives of another soldier and his Eastbourne bride were also wrecked by a V-1. William Jack Brant was the great great-grandson of the famous Mohawk chief, known as Thayendanegea, who had led Iroquois allies of the British during the American War of Independence 168 years previously. The *Hamilton Spectator* reports that Brant's wife and baby were killed at Eastbourne in a V-1 raid. [However, the name Brant is not in the list of the town's air raid casualties.]

Wounded in action twice, he was repatriated and discharged from the forces in February 1945.

However, it was a case of 'happily ever after' for Kay Griffin of Old Town. At the age of 26, she met her future husband, Jack Fennell, at the Winter Garden one Saturday night. Until her death in May 2006, Kay lived in Ontario, where she received frequent visits from her seven children, 15 grandchildren and four great-grandchildren. Jack served with 23 Fd Regt in Meads, and the couple became engaged before the gunners left for Pippingford Park – and thence for Normandy, where they landed on 26 July 1944. Kay did not see Jack again until he got back for their wedding at St Mary's Church in Old Town in March 1945.

One of some 150 marriages of Eastbourne girls and Canadian servicemen took place on 10 March 1945 at St Mary's Church between Jack Fennell from Toronto and Kay Griffin of Old Town. Kay had to wait a further year before getting transport across the Atlantic to start her life in Canada, where she was welcomed with open arms by her new family.

Writing in December 2004, Kay Fennell remembered:

'I crossed in the liner 'Mauritania' in March 1946 and was nervous with anticipation of a new life in a new place. A few of the girls on board the ship exchanged names and addresses but no one ever got around to contacting anyone. The crossing was very good and we had wonderful food – not at all like during the rationing in England. Of course, I was nervous about meeting Jack's family, but I was welcomed with open arms. All of Jack's aunts, uncles and cousins were on the quayside at Halifax to meet me. They were all as nervous as I was.

RMS Mauritania in her wartime dazzle camouflage, which would have been painted out by the time Eastbourne war bride Kay Griffin crossed the Atlantic in 1946. She made the crossing without the discomfort of rough seas, but many of the war brides suffered from seasickness.

Jack lived in a suburb of Toronto and it was nothing like Eastbourne. When we arrived, we took the train from Halifax to Toronto – I'd never seen a station like that before.

I didn't know anything about Canada before I got there. I couldn't believe seeing a Woolworth's store for the first time – full of everything, when the British ones had hardly anything. It was all like something in a dream. There was lots of food in Canada and no rationing at all. The cars were all driving on the wrong side of the road and I nearly got run over a few times because I found myself looking the wrong way for traffic. I never joined a War Brides Association because I was too busy having eight children. I just became a Canadian wife, and didn't look out for English friends.'

On the other hand, another Eastbourne war bride, Enid Granton (née Metcalf), still feels very British and confesses to missing the sea and the Downs, even though she has had a good life in Canada.

Before the war Enid worked at Plummer Roddis in Terminus Road; her father, Percy Metcalf, was an Inspector with the local police. Enid and her mother were evacuated to Cheltenham, but later returned to Bowood Avenue. She then joined the Women's Land Army and was stationed at Lewes. Enid met her future husband on Eastbourne railway station when he asked her what kind of uniform she was wearing – no doubt a popular chat-up line for all servicemen at the time! He was with a Light Aid Detachment of The Royal Canadian Ordnance Corps, and had a lucky escape when his billet in Tideswell Road was narrowly missed by the bomb which fell on Marks and Spencer in Terminus Road on 18 December 1942.

Enid did not see her fiancé from the time his unit went to Italy in June 1943 until their marriage at Our Lady of Ransom in Meads Road in April 1945. In common with most war brides, she had to wait a further year before travelling to Canada. For nearly 60 years, her home has been the small town of Paris in Ontario. When she arrived in 1946 she was surprised to find many women from Yorkshire who had come over between the wars to work in the local textile industry. Furthermore, there were another 25 war brides in Paris (population 5,000) to keep her company.

Reading between the lines of others who lived through the period it is possible – even after 60 years – to detect the glimmer of a torch that still burns. Hearing of this research, a former Wren wrote from London to say: 'I am writing immediately as I am looking for a chap called Rex [surname suppressed] of The Royal Canadian Engineers, whom I had danced with some six weeks before D-Day. He gave me my first 'verbal medal' [kiss] as Wrens like to put it. He said that he came from Regina in Saskatchewan, but can't be found there.'

A gunner of 23 Fd Regt recalls with affection a girl by the name of Joyce: 'Two of my friends and I took it in turns to dance with her at the Winter Garden. We felt she was the best dancer in Eastbourne. She lived at the east end of town in Desmond Road – was that Old Town, or near a district called the Crumbles? I remember there was a nice park nearby, and that it was a long walk back to Meads after seeing her home. Anyway, I remember her so well – a lovely girl.'

Another lovely girl is remembered by Stan Scislowski of The Perth Regiment. She was a pretty Wren, no doubt serving with HMS Marlborough at Eastbourne College:

'Morning roll-calls at Eastbourne were something all of us in D Company looked forward to. Hard to believe, but it was true. Why? Simply because of a fair young maiden, the prettiest thing I'd ever seen, dressed in Royal Navy blue who would pedal by on her bicycle as we were formed up on the street [Dittons Road] *in front of our billets, and give us a big, beautiful smile as she went by. I'm sure every man imagined that smile was directed at him only, not anyone else. This dream girl should have been in Hollywood – she was that pretty.'*

There were 'Popular Dances' at the Winter Garden every weekday evening.

Photograph from the *Eastbourne Gazette* showing dancers at the Winter Garden in November 1941. The caption reads: 'One of the most enjoyable events of the winter season.' The 5th Canadian Infantry Brigade was in the Eastbourne area at the time and so it is likely that men of the Black Watch (Willingdon) and perhaps Le Régiment de Maisonneuve (Pevensey) were present at this dance, which was organised by the British Legion.

Music was often provided by a local band led by drummer, Gordon Rider. Gordon, who was still going strong in the 1960s, gave immense pleasure to thousands of Eastbournians and troops during the war. Veterans recall his last waltz, *Who's Taking you Home Tonight?* As the final notes died away, Gordon would remind the dancers: 'And don't forget your gas masks!'

7
Just one of those things

For every couple who married, there were many more men and women – single and married – who struck up casual relationships. One resident, a teenager in St Anthony's at the time, writes:

'I don't think there were many Canadians left after D-Day as by that time my friends and I were up the seafront most evenings 'picking-up' dozens of soldiers (all very innocent, I hasten to add!) and we never met one Canadian. The only foreigners were the Australians at Chaseley who were brought to Eastbourne from POW camps before being repatriated, and Dutch sailors at HMS Marlborough in the winter of 1945. By the summer of 1946, I don't think there were any servicemen left in Eastbourne – AND LIFE HAS NEVER AGAIN BEEN SO EXCITING! Sorry, I don't wish to give my name or address.'

From the Argus Collection of Newspaper Photographs, State Library of Victoria – former Australian POWs at the Wish Tower in 1945. They were accommodated at Gowrie House, now Chaseley, before repatriation.

The prospect of sudden death and separation could mean that chastity became an early casualty; things got serious and marriages were broken up. In 2003, Babs Clements recalled with classic English understatement: 'One Meads girl was married to a British officer who was a POW, but she still went ahead and bigamously married a Canadian and went off with him. When her husband came home after the war he was quite upset about it!'

'They ain't got nothin' our girls haven't got, only they've got it here!'

This 'Herbie' cartoon by Bing Coughlin is reproduced courtesy of the Canadian Forces. 'Hastings – England' appears below the signature but the scene could be anywhere. The Lance Corporal bears the formation patch of the 1st Canadian Army. It was a standing joke that every good Canuck wanted to own an English pub.

It has not been possible to ascertain the extent of bigamous marriages, but it is known that up to August 1945 ten cases had been prosecuted in military courts nationwide, with a further twelve in British civil courts.[20]

Such matters were taken seriously and the Radio Liaison Officer at the Canadian Military HQ cautioned performers in 'Johnny Canuck's Revue', a variety show broadcast by the BBC and aimed at Canadian forces in Britain. The guidance was that it was better not to refer to relationships between Canadian troops and the girls of this country. The reason being that: 'Jokes may be laughed at at the time, but subconsciously they will contribute to worry in the minds of British troops overseas and to listeners in Canada. They will both be jealous.'[21]

A veteran of The Queen's Own Rifles of Canada [QOR], part of the 8th Infantry Brigade, 3rd Canadian Division, wrote to the author anonymously in November 1988 ending: 'Just call me a Canadian Vet [veteran].' He recalled an incident not at all in keeping with the genteel image of Eastbourne: 'An eating place, open to the street, on the main drag, perhaps, trestle tables and long benches. Lots of food and cheap. Wasn't grand, but filling. And one of the lads furiously groping the waitress with one hand; and this while at the same time eating, North American fashion, with the other. This was in daylight, ten feet from the street. The waitress was very evidently enjoying things to a great degree.'

Unlike the Free French, the average Canadian was not preceded by a reputation for seductive charms – but proof was in the eating and the Canucks would certainly have been something of a novelty to Eastbourne girls. In March 1942, the diarist of the Black Watch writes: 'We are supplying a guard at Birling Gap and when arrangements for billets were taken up with HM Coastguard, we received these answers. "Why! The Army can't come in here; this is government property. Leave my wife alone with Canadian soldiers while I am out on patrol? Not me!"'

In October 1943, the *Eastbourne Gazette* published two letters about soldiers. Although Canadians are not mentioned, it is likely that they form the subject of the complaints. Someone signing 'ANTI-DRUNK' refers to: 'The many cases of drunkenness among young soldiers, their raucous "singing" and bad behaviour for which they are often punished.' However, 'ANTI-DRUNK' comments that publicans should be punished for serving those already under the influence. The second correspondent signs only with initials and makes a more serious allegation:

'My little niece was frightened into hysterics last evening by a soldier who followed her off a bus which stopped at Park Avenue. He caught her up, put his arms around her and

*tried to kiss her, etc. When I tell you that she is only 14
years of age, and small for her age, it may seem worth while
to you to try somehow to shame these men into decent
behaviour. I know they are over here to fight for us, and we
are deeply grateful to them for that, but, at the same time,
they must be made to respect and behave properly to our
young girls.'*

Another concern to both military and civil authorities was an
explosion in sexually transmitted diseases. Eastbourne was no
exception. Unlike in most Canadian provinces, there was initially
no legislation in Britain which required persons known to be
infected with VD to undergo treatment. In the UK, the incidence
of VD among Canadian personnel during the war peaked at 40.6
cases per thousand men in 1943, but fell away due to an education
programme and the departure of troops overseas. However, after
VE Day and the return of troops from the Continent, the figure
rose to 108.3 cases per thousand in the fourth quarter of 1945.[22]

The Council Minutes of the County Borough of Eastbourne
reveal ambivalence about public health warnings. On 26 February
1943 the Chairman of the Sanitary and Public Heath Committee
attended a conference on sexually transmitted diseases in London.
Upon her return, she recommended that notices be displayed in
buses detailing the facilities available for treatment. However, in
April, the Motor Omnibus Committee decided, by five votes to
two, not to allow such information to be displayed. The decision
was challenged, but a meeting of the full Council on 3 May finally
resolved that the town's buses would not display the notices.
Then, on 20 May, the Borough Librarian submitted a set of posters
dealing with the dangers of VD, together with a request from the
Medical Officer of Health that they be displayed in public
libraries. Again, such warnings were not considered appropriate
and the request was refused.

The army was worried about VD and a 1942 order issued in
Eastbourne to the Edmontons had made the position clear:

Increase in VD

During the past month, there has been an increase in the number of men evacuated for VD. Several cases of VDG [gonorrhoea] have been definitely traced as having been contracted in Eastbourne. In none of these cases had prophylactic treatment been obtained at the Blue Light Centre at the Regimental Aid Post. This Blue Light Centre is open 24 hrs a day and treatment is provided offering a very high degree of protection from VD if its services are utilized within six hours of exposure. VD is a very serious matter entailing loss of a man to the army, and most important of all, the possibility of long and painful treatment and the chance of permanent disability.

The Edmonton's War Diary for 4 November 1942 records: 'The American film *Sex Hygiene* was shown again today for personnel of the Battalion who had not seen the film when it was last here.' [If this is the film that the author saw during basic training in the RAF, it would have been a truly horrific experience!] Perhaps this explains the entry for later the same day: 'During the afternoon the Battalion marched out to Map Reference 019176.' This is the junction of the present South Downs Way with the track to East Dean, and here they would witness the finish of the Battalion's cross-country run. Nothing like a brisk route march to take the men's minds off it!*

No correspondents mention a specific red light district, but an address in Bourne Street is declared out of bounds in the orders of various units.

---

*WW2 grid references were based on a different datum from that of today. For this area, the army referred to Sheets 134/5. A reasonable correction for Eastbourne can be obtained by adding 566812 to wartime references. However, this figure is inaccurate for places further afield.

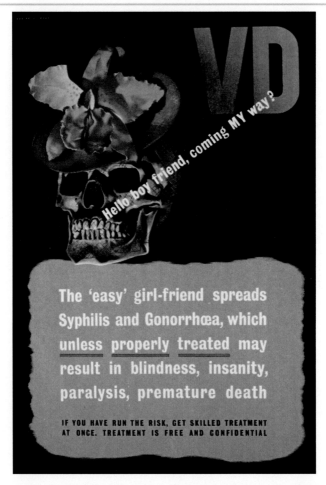

VD has had a pernicious effect on armies through the ages. This 1943 poster from the collection of the Imperial War Museum (PST0800) was created by Reginald Mount and formed part of a campaign by the Ministry of Health. The poster was doubtless one of those considered unsuitable for the town's libraries. Black propaganda services used the fear of VD to demoralise servicemen and civilians alike. The allies played on the fears of German servicemen that their wives might be unfaithful by reporting an epidemic which had allegedly been caused by foreign workers. Similarly, the Germans dropped leaflets on allied troops alluding to an epidemic in the UK.

8
Hands across the ocean

Some residents were concerned when they heard that Canadian troops would be arriving in force. The Black Watch was one of the first units in town and, as part of their responsibility for beach defences, issued permits for fishing and prawning. A CBOE Police Sergeant was among those requesting permission. On 31 July 1941, the War Diary notes: 'The police officer remarked on the behaviour of the Canadians in the town. The inhabitants apparently expected something wild when they heard that the Canadians were coming, but they were obviously pleasantly surprised. This last month has been a very pleasant month, a mixture of work and pleasure, which has done us all good.'

At Christmas in particular, local families would invite men into their homes and hospitality was returned by Sergeants' and Officers' Messes. On Christmas Eve 1941, the Diary of the Calgaries records that civilians in Eastbourne had invited several men to their homes. The Edmontons were in Eastbourne on the day of an air raid on 18 December 1942. This caused heavy casualties to Christmas shoppers in Terminus Road, but was not allowed to interfere with the regimental dance held the same evening – one to which many locals would have been invited: 'The dance during the evening was a great success and everyone seemed to enjoy themselves. The punch (and how it punched) was a concoction of Lt Col J C Jefferson, who believed in getting the party going well from the start. Needless to say there will be some sore heads tomorrow.'

In accordance with army tradition, officers served their men on Christmas Day: 'Turkey, pork, cakes and Xmas pudding. Beer had been bought from the various company funds and all in all the meal proved most enjoyable.' Prior to this, arrangements had been made for the Regiment to entertain children at a party:

'All the officers and many of the men have donated cakes, candy etc which they received in Xmas parcels so the youngsters should have a good feed at last. During the afternoon, certain selected men from each Company and the officers, entertained from 1400 to 1700 hrs the under-privileged youngsters of Eastbourne at a party in the Leaf Hall. They were entertained with musical numbers, community singing and three short movies. The crowning event was when N 16617 Pte Ward A, Chief Little Eagle, appeared in full Indian dress and performed a war dance. The youngsters, many of whom have never seen a Red Indian and probably never will again, were most interested and pleased.'

For the 215 local children who attended, the party must have been a memorable experience.

When talking to locals who remember the Canadian presence, a sense of gratitude comes across strongly – although most did not even realise that all the soldiers were volunteers and not conscripts. However, in some cases, unfamiliar North American attitudes appeared brash and cocky. Antonia Beckett recalls a time when she and her mother passed a newly arrived contingent of Canadians sitting on the grass verge between Victoria Drive and Willingdon Roundabout. They got into conversation and the passing shot from a soldier was: 'Don't worry Ma'am. We're here to win the war for you now!' As Mrs Beckett's sons were also in the services, the remark was not greatly appreciated.[23]

Canadian troops in residential areas had civilians as neighbours. They were under orders not to give – let alone sell – service rations to the folks next door, but a lot of stuff must have been passed over the garden fence. Babs Clements remembered that soap was scarce: 'But one evening, our doorbell rang, and it was some Canadian Sergeants from across the road who had come to bring us soap, wrapped up in a sock. Of course we had them in for a drink.'

The anonymous correspondent of the QOR who describes the goings-on at a restaurant in Terminus Road had arrived in May 1942, when his Regiment relieved the Black Watch:

'The Battalion HQ was a large building [Ratton Wood in Garnet Drive] *but the unit was scattered over a large area. My platoon (Number 10 of B Company) was quartered in a two-storey house* [299 Kings Drive] *near what was known as Willingdon Roundabout. Over our back fence was Westlords Cottage, at that time occupied by a WW1 veteran, his wife and daughter. Morgan was the name, I think.* [Fredrick Morgan is listed in a 1957 *Kelly's* at this address.] *The Morgans were friendly, and we were homesick kids. Some things from the parcels from home went over the fence, and gifts were given back. They were the only family friends we had.'*

French Tricolour and Canadian Maple Leaf fly side by side at the memorial in Bernières-sur-Mer, where troops of the 3rd Canadian Infantry Division came ashore on Juno Beach at 8.05 on D-Day. The Queen's Own Rifles of Canada suffered heavy casualties from machine-gun positions which had survived the naval bombardment. At 8.30 reinforcements arrived including men of another unit which had been in the Eastbourne area – Le Régiment de la Chaudière. One of those on the beach was a QOR soldier who had made friends with his neighbours over the back fence in Kings Drive.

On D-Day, B Company of the QOR landed at Juno Beach in the first wave at Bernières-sur-Mer. The platoon of 'Canadian Vet' numbered 36, but just six remained when they were re-deployed that night. There had been ten men in his section – of these, seven were killed and two wounded.

The inscription on the plaque in front of the house appears in French and in English and reads:

'This house was liberated in first light on D-Day 6 June 1944, by the men of The Queen's Own Rifles of Canada, who were the first Canadians to land on the beach. It may very well have been the first house on French soil liberated by seaborne Allied Forces. Within sight of this house, over 100 men of The Queen's Own Rifles were killed or wounded, in the first few minutes of the landings.'[24]

Most of these casualties would have previously been stationed in Eastbourne. Many – like 'Canadian Vet' – would have made friends with local people. How many local families learnt of the fate of the soldiers they had befriended?

Although Eastbourne is generally remembered with affection by former Canadian soldiers, many veterans mention that as soon as they got some leave, their destination would be Scotland. Perhaps this was because they wanted to make the most of a free rail warrant, but it is true to say that the Scots were generally considered more friendly than southerners. A censorship report for the period 8-21 December 1941 quotes a soldier from a 3rd Division Reinforcement Unit as writing: 'The English are quite friendly but the Scots are more so.' There are several other letters from the same unit to the same effect.[25]

9
Finding Gunner Lawrence

The author's grandparents, Glendale and Clara Mackay, had befriended a Canadian soldier in 1942. He would come to their home at 28 Meads Street and they became quite close. They felt sorry for him, especially as their three boys were themselves away in the forces. The family in Canada wrote expressing gratitude for the welcome given to their son. Over the years, Clara would often talk about the young soldier, but remembered only that his first name was Lawrence, and that via a roundabout route she had later heard of his accidental death following some kind of horseplay. The parents had written from Canada with news of their son's death, but the letter was lost in the raid of Sunday 7 March 1943, when 28 Meads Street was bombed and Glendale Mackay was killed.

In January 2004, a quest – 'Finding Gunner Lawrence' – was started. The first point of reference was Brookwood Cemetery in Surrey, the principal resting-place of Commonwealth and Allied servicemen and women who were killed in air raids or who died of illness or from accidents and wounds – there are 2,405 Canadians of the Second World War interred at Brookwood. The Superintendent confirmed the presence of several with the first name of Lawrence, but before providing details it would be necessary to have the name of a unit.

It was known from the War Diary that the Canadian 2nd Field Regiment RCA [2 Fd Regt] had arrived in Eastbourne in the autumn of 1942, and that by February 1943 their HQ was at Aldro in Darley Road. This seemed a possibility and, sure enough, the Superintendent was able to confirm that a Gunner Lawrence Dempsey of that unit had died on 10 April 1943 at the age of 20. His parents are recorded as P W Dempsey and Mildred Dempsey, of Jacquet River, New Brunswick.

Inquiries in Canada produced a copy of the Court of Inquiry confirming Clara Mackay's recollection. Lawrence Dempsey had died due to paralysis from a dislocation of the vertebrae received during a wrestling bout which had taken place on 7 April 1943.[26] Lawrence had been queuing for breakfast during an exercise on Salisbury Plain. The evidence of the soldier who caused the injury states:

'I was standing by a fire with some other gunners waiting for water to boil for tea. Among this group was the deceased. Gunner Dempsey and myself have been very close friends ever since we joined the army. We came overseas together, and also came to the 8th Canadian Field Battery together. He was doing a batman's job during the scheme and was travelling in the water-wagon of the 8th Battery. It was a habit of ours to frequently have friendly tussles. On the morning of April 7, 1943 Gunner Dempsey in his usual way knocked my hat off. We started boxing and then went to grips together. Dempsey put me down first and then the both of us got up. We went down together again. I returned to my feet but Gunner Dempsey could not. I asked him why he couldn't get up and he replied, "I can't move my arms and legs." The doctor arrived in about five minutes and, under the supervision of the doctor, Gunner Dempsey was put on a stretcher and taken to the ambulance.'

The evidence above is reproduced with the permission of the Dempsey family. The Court of Inquiry concluded that it had been an accident with no evidence of negligence whatsoever.

The Internet revealed Jacquet River to be a small community, with the name Dempsey still listed in the telephone directory. Minutes later a member of the family was giving the address of Lawrence's brother, Patrick, in Florida, who explained that there had been 13 children – he had been Lawrence's elder brother.

Patrick had volunteered for the RCAF and became the Navigator of a Sunderland crew flying to West Africa out of

Pembroke Dock. On the day of the accident he was called to Basingstoke Hospital, where he stayed at his brother's bedside for three days. Lawrence was convinced he would pull through, but doctors had told Patrick there was no hope. He sent a series of telegrams to their parents, breaking the news gently.

Gunner Lawrence Dempsey somewhere in Meads in 1942-3. This young soldier was 'adopted' by Glendale and Clara Mackay, whose home in Meads Street was bombed on 7 March 1943. Glendale died in the raid and Lawrence was tragically killed by a friend during a friendly tussle one month later.

Patrick later met the distraught soldier who had accidentally killed his friend. The young man begged him to take his gramophone and records because they made him feel remorseful and homesick. The wind-up gramophone and 78s ended their days in Africa.

Lawrence Dempsey's parents and Clara Mackay died many years ago, but it is rewarding to have closed the circle after more than 60 years – and finally to have identified 'Gunner Lawrence'.

10
Another day another dollar

The effect of the relatively high-earning Canadians on the local economy should not be underestimated. During off duty hours, many troops in the Upperton area frequented the Tally Ho in Church Street.

Tally Ho – Then
This picture taken on a grey wartime day, and now displayed in the bar of the Tally Ho shows a gunner with greatcoat collar turned up scanning the sky for raiders. Another soldier sets off on a bicycle along Bradford Street with not a car in sight. Note the diagonal strips of paper on the windows to minimise injury from flying glass. Similar machine-gun posts were set up elsewhere in Old Town, above the shops in Albert Parade and on the tower of the Star Brewery.

Norman and Doreen Hodge were licensees of the Tally Ho throughout the war. Doreen commented: 'It was a very good living with all the troops. My son went away at seven to prep school and later to public school. The pub used to be full of Canadians spending loads of money. It was definitely the profits from those years that funded both boys through school.'

Peter Lind of the 31st Battery, 23 Fd Regt singles out the Ship, the Pilot, the Marine, the Sussex and Browns Hotel. The Ship was the local of the 31st and the 36th Batteries, whereas the 83rd Battery favoured the Pilot: 'Any night of the week you would find the Pilot, which was practically a second home for the 83rd, crowded with the lads drinking a few mild and bitters, talking about the present and the past, and listening to the music which Bombardier Stan Watkins poured forth from the piano in the corner'.

Tally Ho – Now
The same view in 2005. The twin Lewis gun is long gone and a ventilation duct now emerges from the rear of the flat roof. The name of the pub – blanked out by the censor – is clearly visible. Little parking space today!

It is hardly surprising that Canadian troops found the traditional English pub an attractive place. Prohibition had come to an end in the Dominion in 1927 and been replaced in Ontario – the Province which provided between a third and a half of all volunteers – by what were called 'beverage rooms'. These were repulsive establishments in which only beer could be drunk, and in which music and any other form of entertainment were banned. No wonder a place where men, and even women, could meet to drink freely what they chose and enjoy themselves was a novel experience.[27]

However, drunkenness was indeed a cause for concern, especially on paydays. The *Eastbourne Herald* of 4 December 1943 reports that the Canadian Army authorities had issued orders to all Sussex publicans that they must not sell spirits to any Canadian servicemen. Mr Justice Charles at Lewes said that any publicans doing so might lose their licences and that their public houses risked being closed.

As the war progressed, what we would now call 'binge drinking' became less of a problem as Canadians came to think of a pub as a place to enjoy themselves, not a place to get drunk. Increasingly they became welcome guests. Already in the summer of 1941, the *Brighton and Hove Herald* reported that the men of 2 Fd Regt [later to come to Eastbourne] had presented a brass plaque to a pub near Brighton in appreciation of hospitality received. The paper commented: 'Is mine host proud of that tablet? I should say he is. "They were just grand guys," he said. "I have had other units in the district; they are all good boys, but somehow they don't think of these things like the Canucks do. I suppose the Canucks are a long way from home and they appreciate a little kindness."'[28]

The *Eastbourne Herald* reported a similar gesture in September 1990, when the three veterans of 23 Fd Regt mentioned on page 21 presented a regimental plaque to the Ship in Meads Street.

The Pilot – Then and Now

Top left – Larry Holleran from St Catherines and Joe Egan from Hamilton about to check out the girls after a Saturday morning drink in 1943. The Pilot was the local for men of the 83rd Battery of 23 Fd Regt.

Above right – the author with Mike Eaton, Manager of the Pilot, at the same spot 60 years on. The stained glass windows remain but their positions have changed.

Left – Larry Holleran on his 80th birthday in June 2004.

PICTUREDROME

THE CINEMA which stood like a rock throughout the aerial bombardment and kept the flag of entertainment flying high in addition to training thousands of troops through the medium of the screen.

Although cinemas were ordered to close from 6 September 1939 for fear that bombing would cause heavy casualties, it did not take the authorities long to realise that entertainment was needed, and most reopened a few days later. The cinema illustrated above is now the Curzon. The Picturedrome and the Luxor subsequently remained open throughout the war; although the Tivoli, the Gaiety, the New Central and the Winter Garden Cinema did eventually close, the latter three reopened in 1942.[29] No doubt they all played to packed houses of civilians and troops. One aspect of wartime picture-going is remembered by several correspondents. Bob Eakin, a veteran of 23 Fd Regt, commented:

'I remember our first trip to the cinema in Eastbourne. The air raid sirens would sound but no one took any real notice until the Cuckoo alarm [local air raid warning] was heard, indicating that enemy planes were directly overhead. The first few times at the cinema were unnerving for us because both warnings would go, and then a notice was flashed on the screen announcing the raid and inviting patrons to leave for air raid shelters, whose locations were indicated. Having just arrived from Canada, we wanted to get up and run for shelter but the English civilians just sat enjoying the picture. So we stayed as well, gripping the armrests tightly – too embarrassed to get up and leave.'

But it was not only cinemas and the licensed trade that benefited from the Canadians. Reginald Smith, who was a greengrocer at 3 High Street, received a welcome contract to supply vegetables for a Canadian unit in the Old Town area. Furthermore, local farmers were grateful for help, especially at harvest time. After all, soldiers from rural backgrounds did not need to be shown how to milk a cow or build a haystack.

In July 1941, when the Black Watch were first in our area, the War Diary records: 'Many of the men who had been farmers left today for a two-week stay with English farmers, whom they are to assist. Whilst this is not a vacation, it will be a change.' The Diary of the Edmontons comments in November 1942:

> *'Apparently the Englishmen still prefer Canadians for farm work for today a request from another source came through for men for farm work. Under the present scheme, men are allowed a week on a farm but receive no wages, other than their usual army pay. They do, however, receive certain luxuries that they normally would not if in camp. The biggest drawing card, so it seems, is the complete change of environment and the men return full of vim and vigour.'*

Troops of the small detachment manning the Beachy Head and Michel Dene Anti-Tank Ranges were based in and around the Birling Gap Hotel, and so lived cheek by jowl with Downland farmers. On 5 July 1943 the CO, Captain Ray Manbert RCA, writes:

> *'A haystack caught fire and this soon got out of control. The NFS arrived, panting with eagerness to have a go at the fire, but had omitted to bring water. The 2nd Anti-Tank Regiment organised a fire-fighting detail and prevented it spreading. The owner of the stack appeared delighted, and departed rubbing his hands and muttering, "£50 for this fire I'll get." The probable cause was spontaneous combustion.'*

11
Marching on its stomach

Stan Scislowski praised our food – in particular the shepherd's pie at Lyons in Terminus Road. His book *Not all of us were Brave* is an account of his service with the Perths in Italy.

Despite the rationing, there are surprising references to both the quality and quantity of food in local restaurants.

The Diary of the Black Watch comments in July 1941: 'Supplies are plentiful here and men are bringing back tales of big juicy steaks, served at a place called 'Snappy Snacks', [sic] which is promising to absorb a fair proportion of the Battalion's payroll.'* The tone is wistful on 17 July: 'The days go by quickly as we are all enjoying ourselves and no one cherishes the thought of returning to the Aldershot area, which it's more or less taken for granted that we do.'

Private Stan Scislowski arrived in England in May 1943 and, after infantry training at Aldershot, joined The Perth Regiment on 5 August. His short stay in Eastbourne was from 14-26 October 1943 – the description of his billet suggests that the house was in Dittons Road.

The Perths had crossed the Atlantic in a convoy to Britain in October 1941, and in January 1943 they were joined by The Irish Regiment of Canada and The Cape Breton Highlanders of Canada to form the 11th Canadian Infantry Brigade. By the time Stan

---

* Snappy Snax, at 3 Albert Parade, was run by a colourful character by the name of Bill Swadling. During the war, he also promoted dances at the Winter Garden. In the 1950s, he was proprietor of the Classic Snack Bar in Terminus Place, and is listed in the 1938 *Pike's* at a snack bar at 8a St Leonard's Road.

reached Eastbourne, the Brigade had secretly been earmarked to take part in the campaign in Italy.[30]

One of Stan Scislowski's memories is of Lyons [opposite the Gildredge]:

'With downtown just a hop, skip and a jump away from our billet [Dittons Road], *all I had to do was walk through the backyard, cut across a soccer field, turn right, walk one short block and I was there. The first establishment you ran into was Lyons. And speaking of Lyons, we found on the first day what gustatory delights we could partake of in this cafeteria-style restaurant. I was surprised to find food here so plentiful, so varied and so delicious. All I'd been hearing since I arrived was how strictly rationed the British were. After my first dinner of shepherd's pie I made up my mind that as long as I had the money, I'd hot-foot it down here to eat, instead of sitting at a crowded table in our own mess trying to put away what our cooks had to serve.*

I spent as much free time downtown as my finances allowed. If I wasn't taking in a movie at one of the cinemas in town, I was just strolling about window-shopping and ogling the eligible female set who chose to stay and face the daily dangers instead of fleeing inland. And there were quite a few, but I wasn't one of the lucky ones to latch on to one of these playmates.'

The former soldier known only as 'Canadian Vet' recalled:

'As growing boys, food was of major importance and army rations were insufficient. The public eating places, somehow, still received rations on a quota based on happier years. We had a weekly 'bath parade' in town. Some of us in the know would hurry to a little tea-room, run by an apologetic old lady. When we asked for lunch, she would say that fish and chips or liver and onions could not be served until midday. However, she could serve us with

bacon, eggs, toast and jam. We always rushed our weekly bath for this. We quartered in Eastbourne in 42, in Shoreham in 43 and Bournemouth in the winter of 43/44. All three were great places to be. But Eastbourne had the best food.'

Even the humble English rock cake proved irresistible to some. Larry Holleran of 23 Fd Regt writes: 'During our morning half-hour break, I would often beat it over to an auxiliary, about half a mile from our location near the Pilot. That's where you could buy rock cakes. Being a 20-year-old I needed the extra rations.' The auxiliary canteen would have been the NAAFI at Tannachie, 46 St Johns Road or at St John's Church Hall.

12
Forget all your troubles – and just get happy

In the same way that the British Army had concert parties as depicted in the TV comedy, *It Ain't Half Hot Mum*, so the Canadians had travelling shows of their own. These included the Tin Hats, the Kit Bags, the Bandoliers and the Forage Caps. All appeared in Eastbourne at various times – at St Elisabeth's Church Hall, the Leaf Hall, the Congregational Hall in Upperton Road and at the Hampden Park Hall, where 500 men of The Princess Patricia's Canadian Light Infantry [PPCLI] crammed in on the night of 27 August 1942 to be entertained by the Bandoliers.

The Tin Hats – the Canadian Army's first official concert party at the finale of their show at the Ambassadors in London in October 1941. Although the performers were not front line troops, they faced danger. During the night of 26 July 1944, the ship carrying them to Normandy was torpedoed. The Tin Hats got off in rafts and a lifeboat – the latter leaked and they had to use their own tin hats as bailers! The casualty summary in the Canadian Army Show lists two performers killed, but there are reports that the number was higher.* The picture is courtesy and copyright the Canadian Department of National Defence.

*Laurel Halladay. "Ladies and Gentlemen, Soldiers and Artists: Canadian Military Entertainers, 1939-1946." Master's Thesis, University of Calgary, 2000.

The Concert Parties also kept War Diaries and these indicate that shows in Eastbourne were generally well received, even though one at the Congregational Hall in Upperton Road in November 1942 did not meet with the approval of the Edmontons: 'The show was not up to the usual standard and the jokes were decidedly on the corny and suggestive side. Strange as it may seem, the troops did not take to suggestive jokes, much to the consternation of the actors, if such they could be called.' The reception must have been a disappointment for the performers, but not as bad as that suffered by the Tin Hats in December 1942. After a performance at the Tudor Close Hotel in Rottingdean for The North Shore (New Brunswick) Regiment, the Concert Party's diarist notes: 'It should be recorded that this Regiment provides the most inattentive and unmannerly audience with which we have ever been in contact!'

LETTING OF ST. ELISABETH'S HALL

"DISREPUTABLE OCCURRENCES OF WHICH WE ARE ASHAMED"

The matter of blue humour had not escaped the attention of the *Eastbourne Chronicle*, which reports on 9 January 1943:

'When the hall has been let for certain concert parties, vulgarities under the name of humour have been thrown across the footlights by alleged comedians, not clever enough to be funny without being low. For these disreputable occurrences we are naturally ashamed and the possibilities of such happenings in a consecrated place must necessarily be put a stop to.'

So it seemed the Church would no longer permit ENSA-type shows at the hall. Instead the Parish would be forming a dramatic club from among its members with the purpose of performing at least three plays every year – at Easter, Christmas and mid-year. However, it is not clear whether these plays were ever performed for the benefit of troops in the area.

This 'shockability' of the troops seems to have been widespread: 'It is sad to have to report that Canadians in general disliked the [British] ENSA shows because they were dirty. We all attended the rankest foulest ENSA show yet. I think we all had nightmares last night.' General MacNaughton, Commander of Canadian Forces in Britain, had voiced his dissatisfaction with the type of show that ENSA [Entertainments National Service Association] was giving which, from his own personal experience, had on occasion been vulgar.[31] Poor old ENSA – the Canadians seemed to have endorsed the alternative meaning of the acronym – 'Every Night Something Awful'!

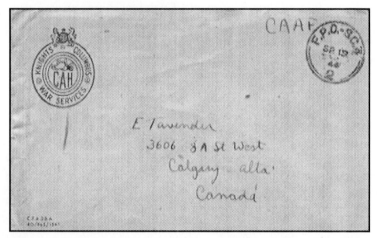

From the collection of Lionel Jones – a serviceman's letter from 1944. CAAF is 'Canadian Army Active Force and FPO stands for 'Field Post Office'. SC indicates that the Post Office was a Canadian static unit, which did not follow the troops. The envelope had been provided by the Knights of Columbus at one of their 'Canadian Army Huts'.

Letters from home were essential for morale, and the Canadian Postal Corps struggled with the difficulties of wartime transport. Letters were lost as U-boats took their toll of transatlantic shipping. The so-called 'armed forces air letters' were later flown across the Atlantic in bombers on delivery from factories in North America.[32] The need for security meant that mail had to be censored, and this delayed mail in the east-west direction. It must have been a temptation for soldiers to circumvent the censor by using red pillar-boxes. A Standing Order of 23 Fd Regt on 29 July 1943 states: 'Civilian letterboxes are not to be used.'

Various service canteens were set up. In December 1941, the Calgaries note: 'YMCA in Langney Road, Eastbourne Churches Social Centre for HM Forces in Langney Road and the NAAFI at YWCA, Hartington Hall, 5 Bolton Road.' In August 1943, the Meads NAAFI was at Tannachie, 46 St Johns Road.

However, Maurice Philipps of The Seaforth Highlanders of Canada [Seaforths] writes: 'The NAAFI was not popular. We preferred our own canteens, which were usually provided by the Sally Ann [Salvation Army].' Eastbourne must have been full of troops in October 1943 for The 19th Field Regiment (SP) RCA comments: 'The local NAAFI has been placed out of bounds because it had been designed for British troops and cannot cope.'

Dissatisfaction with the NAAFI may well have been widespread. Howard Clegg arrived in Britain with the PPCLI in December 1939 and describes his first visit to a NAAFI at an army camp, probably in the Aldershot area:

'We discovered its worst side – namely the personnel. (The serving people are all men – a slovenly looking lot.) They could not have been slower, more unsympathetic and muddling when handing out their wares if they had been feeding an invading enemy. I suppose these NAAFI men, like many of the so-called workmen employed on construction in the barracks, were dragged by the neck from the tail end of the queue of habitual dole-collectors to meet the emergency. At any rate, they seemed to be sour about something. They have given the boys one hell of an impression of our English brethren.[33]

On 21 March 1942, the *Eastbourne Chronicle* reports a new recreational centre at the Leaf Hall under the auspices of the Knights of Columbus. However, it seems this facility was short-lived, for on 28 October 1942 the Edmontons record another ceremony: 'The Auxiliary Services had arranged a canteen and amusement room for the troops at the Leaf Hall and tonight saw the official opening. The hall provides a well-equipped reading and writing room; canteen, amusement room and an upstairs hall for dances and motion pictures.'

This picture, courtesy and copyright the Canadian Department of National Defence, is captioned 'Eastbourne' but gives no location. The decorations suggest that it was taken at Christmas. The photograph above the bar is of Lt-Gen A G L McNaughton, GOC of the Canadian Army.

Four voluntary organisations attended to the recreational needs of Canadians in the UK. Eventually they specialised in certain areas, with the Salvation Army looking after canteens and cinemas, the YMCA responsible for sports and recreation, the Knights of Columbus attending to hospitality and social functions and the Canadian Legion taking over concerts and entertainment.[34]

Troops were encouraged to join part-time educational classes at technical and art colleges. Eastbourne's Technical Institute was chosen as the venue for an exhibition of art and craft by members of the Canadian forces in Britain and was officially opened by Lieutenant General A G L McNaughton, GOC of the Canadian Army on 29 April 1942.

The above painting, *Dawn Alert,* showing an AA gun crew on a beach in southern England is the work of Major Charles Fraser Comfort, an official Canadian war artist. The image (AN 19710261-2178) is reproduced courtesy of the Beaverbrook Collection of War Art, Canadian War Museum © CWM.

The exhibition included some 300 paintings, all of which had been done as a hobby by Canadian soldiers in England; some of the amateur artists had attended classes in the town. At the opening ceremony, the General stressed how important it was for men to be able to continue their education while in the forces.

The Technical Institute stood on the site of the present Central Library in Grove Road, and provided training in practical skills for those local boys who had not been evacuated. Workshops were in the basement, with classrooms and laboratories on the first floor – just as they had been for the Grammar School until the early 1920s.

However, Eastbourne boys were not the only pupils. On Sundays, Canadian troops attended welding classes in the workshops. Some of these men belonged to the PPCLI, who were stationed at the Grange in St Anne's Road. When the Technical Institute was destroyed during an air raid on 7 February 1943, the Commanding Officer of the Regiment proved to be a good friend, for he agreed to make available three rooms at the Grange. This kind gesture turned out to be significant for it would determine the site of what later became Eastbourne College of Arts and Technology (ECAT). In due course, the latter evolved into what is now Sussex Downs College in Cross Levels Way.[35]

Canadians have long been passionate about ice hockey and those in Sussex made good use of SS Brighton, the ice rink then at the bottom of West Street in Brighton. There is a strong tradition of the sport in Montreal, and so is it hardly surprising that a regiment raised in that city – the Black Watch – did well. Their team set out from Meads on 28 January 1942, and returned from Brighton champions of the Canadian 2nd Division, having defeated the 4th Field Regiment, RCA 2-1.

For those favouring a quieter pursuit, honorary membership of the Royal Eastbourne Golf Club was extended to all officers of the 5th Canadian Infantry Brigade in July 1941 – the green fee being fixed at a nominal one shilling per round.[36]

While the Seaforths, from Vancouver, were at Pevensey in November 1942 their Diary records that two officers even rode with the local fox hunt: 'Hoping to keep up the old Western traditions with English saddles on brutes of 17 and 18 hands.'

13
Street fighting

An explosive cocktail of fit young men, testosterone and beer often brings out the worst, and in this respect the Canadian Army was no different from any other. Some did not take kindly to the British Military Police. The former soldier signing anonymously 'Canadian Vet' wrote: 'Our dealings with the British Red Caps were a problem for both sides. We, as volunteers, were not about to be pushed around by what were probably conscripts. There was trouble.'

Bob Eakin of 23 Fd Regt recalled 'Canuck on Canuck' violence: 'For some reason, the 30th Battery of the 6th LAA Regiment RCA had a dislike of our Regiment or Battery. I remember walking home up Meads Road very carefully as a couple of our people had been attacked. The 30th must have been billeted somewhere close to Meads Road, between the Railway Station and Meads Village.' In fact, their HQ was probably Trevin Towers in Gaudick Road, abutting the Golf Links; other likely locations in Meads are Westbrook [now Bishop Carey] and Sunnymead in the same road. Peter Lind of the same Regiment also comments on this LAA unit, which was known as the 'Sportsmen's Battery' and whose Commanding Officer was a celebrity – Major Conn Smythe, owner of Maple Leaf Gardens and Maple Leaf [Ice] Hockey Club in Toronto: 'We would often see well-known athletes in the NAAFI and on the streets or in the pubs of Eastbourne.'

Before joining the RAF, George Humphrey served in the 21st Sussex (Eastbourne) Battalion of the Home Guard, and had first hand knowledge of the conduct of allied troops in the town. He comments:

'While Canadians were a long way from perfect, they were no worse than any other troops and, in most cases, a great deal better. The worst tales about their behaviour

King Haakon Inspects Norwegian Commandos

Number 10 (Inter-Allied) Commando arrived in Eastbourne on 31 May 1943 from Harlech. The Norwegians formed Number 5 Troop. The HQ was at Engedi, 33 St Leonard's Road, with the Troop HQs at Roborough in The Avenue. The men were billeted with local families. In March 1944, in what was the run-up to D-Day, the Inter-Allied Commandos were concentrated at Engedi while another unit, Number 45 Royal Marine Commando, was across the road at Roborough.

generally stem from an occasion when troops of The Irish Regiment of Canada decided to set out on a revenge fight with some Allied Commandos, one of whose men was reputed to have knifed an Irish Canadian in an affray. Nothing came of this because the officers and NCOs of the Regiment pinned the men in their quarters. A row had developed between a small group of some Norwegian Commandos and Irish Canadians outside 'Snappy Snax' on Albert Parade. In the mêlée a Norwegian drew his commando knife and stabbed one of the Canadians. The upshot was that the Canadians returned to their billets and began planning an armed reprisal, but only to be brought to a halt by their NCOs, who searched the buildings and confiscated live ammunition – some of which was found hidden in drains. There is no other case of genuine serious trouble emanating from Canadian troops; they were, in general, exemplary.'

However, another clash between the same troops is recalled by Robert McKee, formerly of The Irish Regiment of Canada:

'I remember talk of a brawl between some members of the Irish and other soldiers of a Commando Group, but have no first hand knowledge of the incident. There was a fight when Canadian soldiers were leaving the Pier Hotel at 10.35 pm on 15 October 1943, the day the bulk of the Regiment arrived. [Billets in and around Prideaux Road] *A Canadian officer was injured and assisted from the scene. Groups of men fought each other and bottles were broken on the street. We were cautioned to maintain friendly relations with the Commandos, who consisted of many nationalities and whose fighting abilities were not to be underestimated.'*

The War Diary refers to neither of the above incidents. However, at muster parades the next morning news came of a different kind of fighting: 'Lt Col Clark revealed the exciting news that the Regiment was to proceed overseas in the very near future. He warned everyone that this was their secret and that it was up to them to keep it a secret. This announcement was received with cheers by every Company. Everyone agreed that this was the best news we had received all year.' On 21 October, their 108 vehicles were assembled in Hampden Park. At 5.05 pm the first train (carrying the advance party with 20 tons of baggage) left Eastbourne station for Liverpool. Two days later the Regiment sailed to Italy.

However, by far the worst case of street fighting did not concern Canadians at all, but British and American troops. On 1 July 1944, Grenadier Guardsman Fox of the British 2nd Armoured Brigade was fatally stabbed outside Snappy Snax on Albert Parade by Juan Marquez, a GI of the 129th Signal Radio Intelligence Company. One month later Marquez was tried by a US Army court-martial and sentenced to be dishonourably discharged from the service, forfeit all pay and allowances and to be confined to hard labour for ten years. However, after the war there was a review of all sentences imposed by US military courts during hostilities, and the Adjutant General, acting under direction from the Secretary of War, remitted that part of the sentence which was in excess of five years.[37]

The GI was based at a secret listening post at Haystoun House in Church Street, Willingdon. The intercept operators and other specialists were billeted at 19 Le Brun Road, 14 Ashburnham Road and at Lynchmere, the former school at the junction of Carew and Ashburnham Roads where Merewood Court stands today. The names of American States can still be seen, carved by GIs in the copingstones of the original boundary wall of Lynchmere.

Also visible in this wall is a smaller inscription, '16 Aug 1944 Pete & Daphne'. Presumably Pete was a GI – but how about Daphne? Was she an all-American girl waiting in the States for her boy to come marching home? Or a local girl who later became a GI bride? Or is Daphne perhaps still in Eastbourne treasuring fond memories of a wartime romance?

14
Read all about it

Security meant that newspapers rarely mentioned the names of units. When the *Eastbourne Herald* published a photograph of the Black Watch in November 1941, the caption refers only to 'the pipers band of a famous Dominion regiment'.

Pipers of the Black Watch accompanying the Mayor, Alderman A E Rush, to St Mary's Church on 22 November 1941.

Similarly, sporting events against local clubs refer only to 'Canadian footballers' although this could also have been because men from various units were included in the teams. However, units are usually identified in the case of weddings. One of the earliest appears in the *Eastbourne Gazette,* which reports the marriage of an officer of the Black Watch at Christmas 1941 – 2nd Lieutenant William Budd – to Miss Mary Bachelor of Sancroft Road.

In the case of crime reporting, it should be realised that – unlike American forces, who appeared before their own service courts – the Canadian military accepted British justice. This state of affairs followed on naturally from the close integration of British and Dominion forces, and the fact that the judicial systems of the two countries were virtually identical. There was also the precedent of the First World War, when the Canadians in the beginning were merely the troops of a self-governing colony, and no one thought of questioning that they were subject to British jurisdiction.[38] Canadians picked up by civil or military police appeared before Eastbourne magistrates; court proceedings were therefore covered in the local press – a state of affairs which cast them in an unfavourable light compared with American troops, whose misdemeanours usually passed unreported.

Statistics prepared by CMHQ in London show that in Surrey and Sussex during the six months ending 5 July 1943, 297 Canadian soldiers were convicted of civil offences – the equivalent of one offender per 12,000 troops per week. These were principally minor affairs such as drunkenness and petty theft. Offences against women totalled 15 – one per 200,000 men per week. Figures from the civil police computed that in Sussex during the first six months of 1943, the average number of offences against women per 10,000 troops was 7 for British troops, whereas the figure for Canadians was 3.22. [39]

ALLEGED ROBBERY WITH VIOLENCE

CANADIAN SOLDIER REMANDED

WOMAN COMPLAINS OF ASSAULT AND SNATCHING OF HANDBAG

In court, British magistrates frequently erred on the side of leniency when faced with a Canadian accused of a mild misdemeanour, taking the view that a young man had crossed the Atlantic to help Britain in her hour of need and that a severe sentence would be inappropriate.

74

However, this happened so frequently that Canadian officers felt leniency had gone too far and that the law provided an insufficient deterrent to wrongdoing.[40]

The *Eastbourne Chronicle* reported that on 17 December 1941, a 23-year-old Canadian based at Pevensey, and so presumably a member of the Maisonneuves, had been remanded in custody in connection with an accusation of robbery with violence which had taken place at around 11.30 pm in Churchdale Road. The proceedings were conducted with the aid of an interpreter and reported in the press.

A wartime picture of Eastbourne Bus Station in Churchdale Road. A former policeman, working here as a cleaner, heard a woman's cries for help and apprehended a Canadian soldier, who later appeared before the magistrates on a charge of assault.

At the subsequent hearing on 29 December, a widow from Willoughby Crescent alleged that the soldier had grabbed hold of her and kissed her down the right side of the face. While she was trying to get away, he heaved her over a hedge and came down on top of her on the grass. Fortunately a cyclist came past and she was able to call for help. The soldier then made off with her bag, which contained around £1 in cash, together with a post office savings book and a pension order book.

The soldier was pursued by a cleaner from the bus depot, who knocked him out when he failed to stop. The soldier, who had been drinking, maintained that he had met the woman in the Alexandra Arms and given her five shillings. He said that she had later offered to sleep with him for a pound, but he had told her that he did not have a pound and demanded his five shillings back. Having heard all the evidence, the magistrates reduced the charge from robbery with violence to one of larceny, and fined the soldier £5.

In May 1942, the *Eastbourne Chronicle* reported that magistrates had heard an accusation of armed robbery on the part of two Canadians. It was alleged that they had robbed a local man of £1 at an address in Seaside while armed with a revolver and a broken bottle. However, the case was dismissed owing to insufficient evidence. The bench was of the opinion that the incident was part of a drunken brawl, and the men were advised to limit their drinking.

Such leniency did not apply in October 1943, following a charge of breaking and entering at St John's Parish Hall in Meads, part of which was used during the war as a service canteen. In this incident, cigarettes, tobacco, cigarette papers, razor blades, toothpaste and shaving soap were stolen. The soldier, described by the *Eastbourne Chronicle* as being a member of the Canadian Reinforcement Unit [a holding unit], was committed for trial at Sussex Assizes.

Soldiering is a dangerous business in wartime – even in a friendly country and far from the enemy. Of the 2,405 Canadians buried at Brookwood Military Cemetery in Surrey, a large proportion met their deaths in traffic accidents, many of these occurring during the blackout. At greatest risk were the motorcycle dispatch riders – indeed the cemetery was ironically known as the 'dispatch rider holding unit'. Such fatalities were routinely investigated by British coroners and reported in the local press.

The *Eastbourne Chronicle* reported that on 18 July 1942, a motorcycle dispatch rider, Signalman Chester Wintle, had been killed when he was hit by an army lorry in Seaside. Further details are given in the War Diary of the 8th Canadian Infantry Brigade [HQ Crossways House, Upper Dicker], which states that Signalman Wintle had been on a regular dispatch run. The 22-year-old motorcyclist was almost certainly on his way to Le Régiment de la Chaudière [Chaudières] at Stone Cross or Pevensey, and may well have been killed by one of this unit's 30cwt trucks as it turned across his path into Seaville Drive.

Another fatal road accident had earlier been covered by the same local newspaper. On the night of 10 April 1942, a Canadian officer and a sergeant were walking between Wilmington and Polegate when they were hit from behind by another Canadian on a motorcycle. The motorcyclist and the sergeant were injured and the third man, Lieutenant John Poulton, was killed. The Canadian National Archives in Ottawa indicate that Poulton had emigrated from Britain in 1921 and joined The Royal Canadian Navy before taking a job with a telephone company. He had enlisted in the South Saskatchewan Regiment in 1939, and volunteered to serve overseas in the defence of his country of birth.

CANADIAN OFFICER KILLED

KNOCKED DOWN AT NIGHT BY ARMY MOTOR CYCLIST

MATTER FOR MILITARY COURT OF INQUIRY, SAYS CORONER

The same newspaper reported an accident on 11 July 1941. Rifleman John Drader was scrambling to get on a lorry when one of his comrades threw a loaded rifle into the back causing it to discharge. A bullet hit Draper in the back. Recording a verdict of accidental death, the Eastbourne Coroner commented on the soldier who had caused the fatality: 'I think he was guilty in some degree of carelessness in throwing this loaded rifle into the back of the lorry – not that it affects the verdict.' Inquiries in Canada reveal that the victim was with The Royal Winnipeg Rifles.

With the stress of wartime, and arms and ammunition to hand, a number of soldiers took their own lives. There were 93 suicides among men of the Canadian army in Britain during the war, the figure peaking at 27 in 1942.[41] Although the house is not cited in the newspaper, it is known that one case was at Compton Court in Dittons Road. The *Eastbourne Chronicle* reported on 25 October 1941:

CANADIAN N.C.O. TAKES HIS OWN LIFE

HAD BEEN ASKED TO ATTEND AT ORDERLY ROOM TO BE INTERVIEWED BY HIS C.O.

CONSCIENTIOUS AND SENSITIVE, AND, MIGHT HAVE BEEN NEEDLESSLY WORRIED OVER "QUITE A SMALL MATTER"

Canadian documents reveal that the NCO was in D Company of The Toronto Scottish Regiment (MG), which formed the Support Battalion of the 2nd Canadian Division. He owed a small sum of money to another man and was due to be interviewed. His CO told the Coroner that he would have been told to repay the debt in instalments. Sergeant C J Arnold of the Eastbourne Police said that he had been called to Compton Court on the morning of 20 October. In a bedroom, he found the body of the NCO, who had shot himself through the head with his service rifle. The bullet had penetrated the wall and was found in the next room.

The Inquest was told that the soldier had been of a cheerful disposition, but very conscientious and over-sensitive. No note had been left.

Compton Court in Dittons Road was quarters for the Toronto Scottish Regiment. In one of the bedrooms, a Canadian Lance Corporal took his own life with a service rifle in October 1941. Other houses in the road were also used by British and Canadian forces, the Home Guard and the Royal Navy. These included Dunvegan, Roselawn (HQ of the local Home Guard) and Park Gates.

Not that the reporting of Canucks in Eastbourne was all one way – Eastbourne is mentioned at least once in the Canadian press. In August 1942, a question in the House of Commons by the town's MP, Major Charles Taylor, about saluting in London was reported by the *Hamilton Spectator* in Ontario complete with a stereotype cartoon. A body of feeling had been growing in Britain that saluting should be dispensed with in places like Aldershot and London because of the frequency with which soldiers and NCOs encountered officers.

Major Taylor had sought clarification, and was cheered in the House when he queried the desirability of any relaxation in military regulations.

Major Taylor said: 'If it is argued there should be a slackening of the rule because of a salute every twelve paces, the whole thing should be set out officially.' Within 24 hours of his question, a British national newspaper featured a cartoon showing a Tommy reading a newspaper article headed: 'MP complains not enough saluting', and saying to a sailor: 'Perhaps that's what's wrong in the Don Valley, pal!'

As a follow-up to the above, the Ontario-based cartoonist, Bill Freyse, produced the above caricature for the *Hamilton Spectator*.

15
Frenchies

The normal establishment of the British and Canadian armies was three infantry battalions to a brigade. There had been an attempt to create a totally French-speaking 5th Brigade consisting of the Royal 22e Régiment ['Vandoos'], Les Fusiliers Mont-Royal and Le Régiment de Maisonneuve. However, this never came about; the Royal 22e Regiment was moved to the 3rd Brigade and Les Fusiliers Mont-Royal [later suffering heavy casualties at Dieppe] to the 6th Brigade.[42]

French Canadian units in this area were Le Régiment de Maisonneuve and Le Régiment de la Chaudière. Outside Quebec, the poster read: 'Come on Pal – Enlist!' It was designed by Henry Eveleigh and appears courtesy and copyright the Canadian War Museum.

Of the proposed Francophone components of the 5th Canadian Infantry Brigade, only the Maisonneuves, from Montreal, remained. They were joined by another regiment from that Quebec city – the predominately English-speaking Black Watch. The third element was the Calgaries, who hailed from the Province of Alberta. The Black Watch – the oldest Canadian Highland regiment – had better facilities in Montreal than the Maisonneuves, who first had to share an armoury with an artillery unit and were then quartered in poor conditions at a converted factory. However, despite these disadvantages there was certainly no shortage of volunteers for the Maisonneuves – more than 2,000 men enlisted in the first week of September 1939, before Canada was officially at war.[43]

The Maisonneuves were led by Lieutenant Colonel Robert Bourassa, a Great War veteran, who was a Crown Attorney prominent in Montreal legal circles, and the third generation of his family to serve in the Regiment. Bourassa was not an easy man for the Canadian army to deal with. He was taking a refresher course for field officers when word came that war was imminent. Reaching Montreal on August 25, he quickly became involved in a bitter dispute over the command of guards posted in the city. The men were Maisonneuves, but the officers were English-speaking, and artillery to boot. Bourassa would not accept this injustice both to his Regiment and to French Canadians, and a long battle of words ensued. The French-language newspaper *Le Devoir* commented indignantly that the Regiment was being denied space for offices and training by 'un régiment de langue anglaise'.[44]

The 5th Canadian Infantry Brigade sailed for the UK in August 1940, and moved at once to Aldershot. Sadly, on the evening of their arrival, Lieutenant Colonel Bourassa was rushed to hospital with what turned out to be a brain tumour; he would never see his Regiment again. Major Paul Brosseau, the second-in-command, took over the next day.[45]

The Canadian Army overseas was essentially one of volunteers, and those from the French-speaking Province of Quebec were proportionally fewer in number compared with other parts of the Dominion. The Quebecois had no ties with Britain; indeed there was even a certain amount of anti-Gaullist and pro-Vichy feeling in the Province. Conscription was firmly resisted by Quebec Francophones who saw no reason to be forced to fight overseas in causes which had little to do with them.[46]

Even after the entry of the United States into the war and the threat posed to Canada's coasts, this attitude did not change to any great extent. Furthermore, Canada's small regular army had only

5% of Francophones before the war, and there was accordingly little tradition of military service within this group. Yet, despite all of this, nearly 150,000 Francophones did volunteer – 85,000 to 90,000 from the Province of Quebec. As the army had few French Canadian units, some 3,000 Francophones were incorporated into English-speaking units. It is hard to be precise on how many French-speaking Canadians joined up because it was not a requirement to state racial origin or mother tongue.[17]

In their quarters in Meads, the mood among men of the Black Watch was sombre at the beginning of 1942. The expected Japanese assault on Singapore was reported on 8 February and the Diary reports gloomy comments about the recruiting situation from an officer just back from Canada:

'He was speaking mainly of Quebec although the general spirit of apathy seems to be in evidence in other provinces. According to his reports, all sorts of inducements and persuasive measures are resorted to in order to gain recruits for active service but still the flow of recruits is only a dribble. Certainly this is not a situation calculated to cheer the Canadians over here.'

Local residents recalling the war express gratitude for the help that was forthcoming from the Dominion. Yet it has to be said that some voiced mixed feelings about the French Canadians, even though it appears that few were ever based in Eastbourne itself. There would have been language difficulties, and these may explain a comment which has been heard several times: 'The French Canadians had a chip on their shoulder.' On the other hand, the War Diary of the Maisonneuves, who were sent to the Sussex coast in the summer of 1941, makes it clear that the detachment was appreciated by troops and residents alike.

The Maisonneuves became the first French Canadian unit in the Eastbourne area, arriving in Pevensey from Aldershot at the beginning of July 1941. As previously stated, they formed part of the 5th Canadian Infantry Brigade with the Black Watch at

Willingdon and the Calgaries in Upperton. The move, while not exactly planned as a summer holiday, was seen as a way to boost morale for troops who had become disenchanted with life in garrison towns such as Aldershot.

The War Diary is written in French, but orders from Brigade appear in English alongside those in French generated at Battalion level. This often results in a mixture of two languages within a single sentence, as for example: 'Le Lieutenant Massue a passé avec grand succès un cours de Driving and Maintenance.'

Although many officers and NCOs of the Maisonneuves had a knowledge of English, the same was not necessarily the case for other ranks. As far as the rest of the 5th Canadian Infantry Brigade is concerned, the Black Watch from Montreal, a city with a large number of English speakers but situated within Francophone Quebec, would have included men proficient in both languages. However, the Calgaries, from Alberta, would have been almost exclusively English speakers.

The War Diary of the Maisonneuves opens at Pevensey on 8 July 1941, and provides an unusually detailed account of a regimental deployment. Battalion HQ was in a requisitioned house adjacent to the Castle; the Signals Office was within the Castle walls. In the event of an invasion, the ancient fortification would become the Battle HQ, and was well suited for this purpose with rooms and cellars providing ideal storage for munitions. Observation posts on the ramparts commanded a view of shore positions; machine-gun posts were set up within the massive walls. The Officers lodged at the Priory Court Hotel, which had been taken over as their Mess. From time to time, passers-by would call demanding lunch or afternoon tea, unaware that the hotel was now in military hands.

The HQ Company was in huts and abandoned houses in the centre of the village. The Regiment's A Company formed a reserve for the three others, which were deployed along the shoreline. Two of its three platoons were in Westham – one at the western edge of the village and another in the centre – the third was near Pevensey Bay Halt. It was the task of A Company to guard the HQ and patrol the villages at night. B Company was at Langney Point, in rudimentary accommodation at what had been the Isolation Hospital. This is described as a bleak location on the shore, over a mile from the nearest habitation and made even more inhospitable by surrounding minefields. The Diary notes that the mines were extremely sensitive! [During a subsequent detachment to Pevensey in March 1942, one of their men was killed when he strayed into a minefield.] B Company's Reserve Platoon was set back along the road between Eastbourne and Pevensey Bay.

C Company occupied a central position facing the sea at the junction of the road from Pevensey to Pevensey Bay, its men in houses abandoned by their pre-war owners. D Company, on the beach at the eastern edge of Pevensey Bay, had struck lucky as far as billets were concerned: *'Les quartiers les plus confortables et luxueux occupés par le Régiment'*. These small houses had also been abandoned – now three or four soldiers were allotted to each. Personnel of the Reserve Platoon were accommodated in huts which had been erected on farmland.

The Regiment's B Echelon comprised the Quartermaster and his staff, and the Transport Platoon; this was positioned seven miles inland just outside Hailsham. The main building here was a depot built by the War Department and included offices, storage units, garages and workshops. The troops were quartered in huts around the main depot. The Bren Carrier Platoon and its tracked vehicles were to the west of Polegate in 'charming little houses deserted by their former occupants'. The various sections of this platoon were up to a mile and a half apart.

The area met with general approval, and the troops enjoyed a welcome break among friendly people who had nevertheless felt a certain apprehension when warned that Canadians would be coming. The War Diary states that both sides would part as friends.

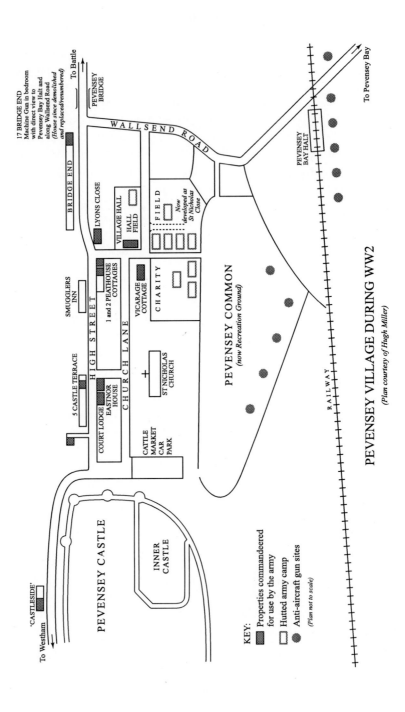

PEVENSEY VILLAGE DURING WW2

(Plan courtesy of Hugh Miller)

KEY:

- Properties commandeered for use by the army
- Hutted army camp
- Anti-aircraft gun sites

(Plan not to scale)

PEVENSEY CASTLE

INNER CASTLE

'CASTLESIDE'

To Westham

5 CASTLE TERRACE

COURT LODGE
EASTNOR HOUSE

CATTLE MARKET CAR PARK

ST NICHOLAS CHURCH

CHURCH LANE

HIGH STREET

SMUGGLERS INN

1 and 2 PEATHOUSE COTTAGES

VICARAGE COTTAGE

CHARITY

LYONS CLOSE

VILLAGE HALL

HALL FIELD

FIELD

Now 'developed as St Nicholas Close

BRIDGE END

17 BRIDGE END
Machine Gun in bedroom with direct view to Pevensey Bay Hall and along Wallsend Road
(House since demolished and replaced/renumbered)

WALLSEND ROAD

To Battle

PEVENSEY BRIDGE

PEVENSEY COMMON
(now Recreation Ground)

PEVENSEY BAY HALT

RAILWAY

To Pevensey Bay

On the evening of 16 July, a dance was organised by the Canadian lay order, the Knights of Columbus. The evening was a great success, thanks in no small part to the presence of many girls whose employers had agreed to send them along.

Perhaps it was through the Knights of Columbus that Lt Charles-Auguste Begin of the Maisonneuves met Antoinette Talibart, whose father had long been a teacher of French in Eastbourne. In any event, their wedding at Our Lady of Ransom is reported in the *Eastbourne Chronicle* in February 1942, together with a note that the bride would be working for the lay order. The Regiment's War Diary records that Lt Begin was the first of their officers to marry in the UK.

It is known that shop assistants were bussed to Meads for dances at St John's Parish Hall, and so it is probable that the girls attending the function at Pevensey for the Maisonneuves would have worked at department stores. In those days, female staff members were often accommodated in hostels and subject to strict discipline. Single girls at Plummer Roddis (now 72-90 Terminus Road) lived in the staff hostel above 106 South Street.

The men were sorry to be ordered back to Surrey in the middle of August 1941. However, they were to return for a longer detachment on 14 October of the same year.

The Regiment was still in Pevensey at Christmas 1941, but by 1 May 1942, their HQ had been moved to Mill Farm at Hankham. However, even from here they were still involved in defence duties along the shoreline. Residents of Pevensey speak of a spectacular fire on the outskirts of the village. Hugh Miller of Westham recalls: 'While French Canadians were based in the Thatched House, a spark from their fire ignited the thatch and the whole building was destroyed. I remember watching the huge blaze and related events from my bedroom window.'

Other French Canadians are remembered by a former resident of St Anthony's, who writes: 'I lived in Rotunda Road and all the empty houses had been evacuated. I think it was early 1942 when the first troops arrived. They were there for a short time, and belonged to a French Canadian regiment – it sounded like 'Chau-de-aire' – they were very unpopular!'

The above would have been other Québécois – Le Régiment de la Chaudière, part of the 8th Infantry Brigade, Canadian 3rd Division. They were based at Stone Cross although some men were billeted at the eastern end of Eastbourne due to a shortage of accommodation in the village. The Chaudières were also involved in the defence of the shoreline at Pevensey Bay. According to Maurice Phillips of the Seaforths, who were part of the 2nd Infantry Brigade, Canadian 1st Division, his Regiment relieved the Chaudières in August 1942.

Maurice Phillips went on to marry a Women's Land Army girl staying in Mill View Close, Westham; his own billet was some 400 yards south of the Red Lion, on the road towards Friday Street. He writes: 'We were discouraged from going into Eastbourne except for catching a train for leave.' This same restriction would have applied to the Chaudières, and accordingly the presence of these French Canadians in the town would also have been limited.

Jacqueline Lloyd-Davies has fond memories of French Canadians [probably Chaudières] who were billeted in the Baldwin Avenue and Milton Road area in the run-up to D-Day.

'One afternoon, my mother introduced me to a young French Canadian soldier with my aunt who had volunteered to billet him with the family for a short duration. Several people in the neighbourhood had also offered to accommodate between 30 and 40 young French Canadians. The young man in question was no more than 18 or 19 years of age, but looked hardly more than a boy.

From the collection of Mark W Tonner of London, Ontario – a shoulder title of the French Canadian regiment which landed on Juno Beach on D-Day. The people of Bernières were delighted to be confronted with men who spoke their own language.

Very soon, whole groups of young soldiers were visiting us on a regular basis and we became firm friends. All of them laughed delightedly at our attempts to speak French and also at our pathetic pronunciation.

My mother and I baked cakes especially for them when they visited. They told us about their families and we exchanged addresses, vowing to write after the war. Little did we know that these handsome young men would soon be sent to France on D-Day and that out of the group we met personally, only one would return to give us the tragic news that the rest had been killed. How sad we were to hear this news. We all shed tears for these brave young men. To this day, I will always remember them – their youth and the love we all felt for them and they for us.'

16
In the field

Emphasis was placed on training – apart from anything else, periods of inactivity made the men stale and restless. Small arms firing was carried out at the long-established Crumbles Rifle Range, but additional temporary ranges were set up at Tas Combe behind Chalk Farm at Willingdon and at land around Haywards Bottom and Half Bottom to the west of Street Farm at Jevington. However, the range which appears to have had the greatest use was what the Canadians called the Holywell Range at Whitbread Hollow. The targets were near the cliff edge and sentries were posted to ensure range safety. Trenches near the cliff-top path were still visible in the 1950s and these may have been the butts for this range. There are also references to cliff scaling exercises at this point.

As part of an exercise on the evening of 21 November 1941 seven men of C Company of the Black Watch staged a surprise attack from the beach against their own A Company, who were defending the Bandstand. The War Diary notes:

'They managed to wriggle and cut their way through the wire and get up onto the promenade which formed the sentries' beat. Inasmuch as the rest of A Company were forming a large (and decidedly partisan) audience it was not possible for the attackers to complete the proposed attack and disarm the sentries: the sentries became aware that the 'enemy' were close beside them and challenged. However, it was a splendid object lesson in the necessity for alertness and will probably serve as a caution to the men manning the waterfront posts. For C Company it was a good piece of practice work for the type of thing they hope to be called upon to do shortly.'

In addition to training at regimental level, many large-scale exercises were held in southern England during which units would leave town for days on end. One of the toughest was 'Exercise Tiger' organised by General Montgomery, whose inspection of the 5th Canadian Infantry Brigade included a brief and unannounced visit to the Black Watch at Willingdon on 3 March 1942. The War Diary comments that he struck them as living up to his reputation as a man of action and decision. Monty's own notes record that he found them a fine battalion with good officers. However, he considered the NCOs patchy, and was scathing in his assessment of their new CO.[48]

During 'Exercise Tiger', the armies of Sussex (No 1 Canadian Corps) and Kent (British No 12 Corps) fought across southern England for eleven days from 19 to 30 May 1942. This was a truly massive operation during which thousands of men from 15 brigades were supported by aircraft, tanks and all manner of vehicles.[49]

The Black Watch left their billets at Willingdon for 'Exercise Tiger' on 14 May, after which they went under canvas at Pulborough until the exercise got underway. The entry in their War Diary for 29 May 1942 shows that even gruelling training schemes could have a lighter side.

'The Battalion took up a defensive position in the village of Lenham [Kent] *and had no sooner done than four Valentine tanks* [24th Lancers] *came storming through the village and left everyone absolutely dumbfounded. A minute later more were heard coming and, brilliant improvisers, the Black Watch took an enemy vehicle, which had been put out of action the previous night by an umpire, and pushed it into the path of the advancing tanks. The leading tank made no attempt to stop but careened right into it and stove the side on the 15cwt truck in! The owner of the vehicle, a British officer, turned green and began to splutter that someone would have to pay for this! Once stopped, the tanks were simply surrounded. The tank crews suffered very rough handling from the Black Watch stalwarts. If there is one*

lesson learnt from 'Tiger', it is that no one in this Unit will ever have any great fear of a tank again. In all we were credited with 13 tanks completely destroyed.'

The War Diary of the unit which had replaced the Black Watch at Willingdon in May 1942, the QOR, gives further insight into the conduct of these large-scale exercises. Before embarking on 'Tiger', the QOR had only just completed another scheme, 'Beaver IV', at the end of which they had fought their way into West Dean after a river crossing at Exceat. Following a short breather they advanced up the Downs towards Friston accompanied by tanks. At 1600hrs on 13 May, 'Beaver IV' was declared over and the next day the exhausted troops marched to the billets which had been vacated by the Black Watch. These were around Willingdon Roundabout and Park Avenue, with the BHQ at Ratton Wood at the top of what is now Garnet Drive. The QOR's War Diary records:

'Blistered feet and fatigue were forgotten and the men, who all knew something of the billets they were to take over, got busy cleaning themselves up. The Unit set about settling down to such comfortable quarters with enthusiasm and hoped that the big scheme 'Tiger' might not materialise, or at very least, hoped it might be delayed. A forlorn hope!'

Before the start of such exercises, troops would move to concentration areas, often in woodland which provided cover for men and vehicles. Less than a week after the end of Beaver IV, the QOR were assembling for the start of Exercise Tiger in Abbots Wood near Arlington. According to the War Diary, this had appeared on the map as a huge wooded area, but many trees had since been felled. It must therefore have been difficult to get some 800 bodies and vehicles under cover.

The main bulk of the troops and equipment arrived in the woods from Willingdon during the early hours of 20 May, and managed to snatch a few hours' sleep under the trees: 'As dawn broke the fog lifted and the sun shone through the oaks to reveal the tired unshaven faces of sleeping men in the mass of bluebells which covered the ground. A strange contrast.' Later that day, most of them turned up at the Old Oak at Arlington where they proceeded to drink the place dry! The Regimental History goes on to describe what the next eleven days held in store:

'Exercise 'Tiger' was a South-Eastern Command exercise and quite the biggest affair of the year. As is usual in exercises, the weather, on the whole, was execrable; the food fitful in arriving; and sleep highly irregular. Two of Monty's ideas tried out in the exercise were that a man could do nicely on two meals a day; and that no man should be asked to carry more than forty pounds, including his boots and clothing. Needless to say, the troops endorsed the second idea with more fervour than they did the first. So much talk about mechanisation made many at home think that transport was always available. True it is that the battalion had transport. Little was used, however, in lifting the troops. They marched everywhere. During these manoeuvres, three marches were made of 35, 37 and 28 miles. It needs little imagination to appreciate that when on 2 June 1942, the battalion dragged its blistered and bleeding feet back to Eastbourne, the sight of that town was very welcome indeed.[50]

'Exercise Tiger' ended on 1 June 1942, when the attention of the QOR turned to securing beach defences and minefields in Eastbourne: 'For the most part the mines could not be seen but in places the beach shingle had shifted causing them to be exposed. It seemed that to cross these fields even in daylight an invader would have a perilous task. Miles of tubular scaffolding, tangled barbed wire, tank blocks and mines seemed to form a formidable rampart to the towns and countryside.' There were also beach lights along the seafront: 'These were thought to be in need of attention but there seems to be some doubt as to who is responsible.' The Intelligence Section reconnoitred the beach to Cow Gap, from where the path led to the cliff top near one of the radio-location [radar] stations. This was considered a vulnerable point that needed strengthening against sea-borne raids, especially as a German E Boat had been reported off Beachy Head at night. Further to the west, the wire at Birling Gap was in poor condition.

At the town end of the beach defences, the QOR received a request from the RAF for a section of wire to be cleared near the Bandstand to allow sea bathing for personnel at the Cavendish Hotel. However, this was not approved as it was felt it might attract hit and run raiders. The Diary states: 'Bombs might hit the large hotels on the waterfront in which the RAF personnel are billeted and cause heavy casualties. In a recent raid a hit was scored on one of these, killing four air force men. Had the raider scored a hit 20 minutes earlier, 250 men would have been in the part of the building completely demolished by the bomb.' This is a reference to the raid of 4 May 1942 when aircrew cadets at the Cavendish Hotel happened to be out on a sports afternoon.[51]

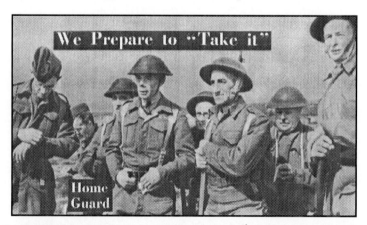

Lt Freddie Morris and men of C Company, 21st (Eastbourne) Battalion at the start of an exercise. Between 19 June to 21 June 1942, they trained with the QOR in Exercise Fox, during which they were put in trenches and fire from machine-guns was laid down over their heads. The Canadian War Diary comments: 'The HG took a poor view of this and explained that they already knew what it felt like to have bullets overhead from rifle range practices.'

The QOR Diary also refers to 'Exercise Fox', a local scheme with the Home Guard which took place from 19 to 21 June 1942. This culminated in an assault on the town by sea at midnight by C Company of the QOR. The Canadians were assisted by the Coastguard, who provided a boat. The Diary continues:

'This was a fishing boat described as being none too safe when loaded with two sections plus their arms. The remainder of the Company 'landed' in theory and attacked the beach, cutting wire in places and attacking posts at the Redoubt, West Bandstand and other points. The attack was said to be successful but would not have been had the HG placed patrols along the wire at dark. Beach lights were used successfully but could not be used directly along the beaches for fear of showing too much to an enemy E Boat reported off shore. At 2345 the 21st Sussex HG, thinking the whole of the Battalion was still in the Willingdon billets, attacked Battalion HQ in Willingdon.'

The equivalent of the Home Guard was the Veterans Guard of Canada. They guarded factories and POW camps. © CWM

During the afternoon of 21 June, the QOR received orders to advance on the Town Hall from the Downs. They were given a route free of enemy, but in the descent a wrong turn was taken with the result that two 15cwt trucks ran into an enemy position. Shots were exchanged, but the raiders reached the Town Hall, where a temporary HQ was set up. Companies then converged on the centre of the town to attack the Wish Tower. However, before this could be reached, the scheme was declared over. A conference was held at Willingdon that evening between officers of both sides and the umpires. The conclusion was that the QOR had suffered heavy casualties and that a concentrated drive into any part of the defences with a fanning out movement once inside would take the town. The western side, on the slopes, was deemed the weakest spot.

It is interesting to read the view of one of the 'enemy'. George Humphrey was a youthful member of the 21st Sussex Home Guard at the time and took part in Exercise Fox as a defender. His memories of that night are vivid:

'Exercise Fox was the 'punch line' at the end of a fortnight of exchanges between the QOR and the 21st Sussex (Eastbourne) Battalion. Our C Company were at Ratton with C Company of the QOR. Here we were taken through live ammunition 'Battle Drill', during which the Canadians poured rifle-calibre stuff across a shallow trench in which we lay. We impressed them with our calmness, but they had not reckoned with the fact that we had been bombed and machine-gunned more times than enough. Our Battalion was to occupy its perimeter battle positions and stand by to repel attacks by the QOR. We were 'attacked' by Curtiss Hawk fighters of the RCAF, and Canadian patrols moved close to our position to try to draw fire and gauge our firepower and dispositions, but we would not be drawn.

During the night the Canadians blew a hole in the beach defences. However, by this time, I had one section in the basement area of the Belle Vue Hotel, one in the Carpet Gardens, which at that time were filled with onions rather than flowers, and part of the third section on the shelter to the east of the pier. HQ personnel and the automatic weapon of Number 3 Section were with me in the entrance.

When the Canadians rushed at the Pier entrance, they were caught by fire from three sides. As the range shortened I ordered a cease-fire because at 15 feet, blank cartridges can inflict nasty burns.

This interesting shot showing the gap in the pier was taken by Bob Hurst of Toronto in 1942. Note the scaffolding barrier and barbed wire in the shrubbery. In the run-up to D-Day, assault craft were parked beneath south coast piers, and camouflage netting draped around the iron stanchions to conceal the boats from enemy aircraft. Men of the Royal Canadian Engineers rigged up the netting. In February 1943, a sapper fell into rough seas and was seriously injured when he struck girders in the fall. Two comrades dived to his assistance, and all three spent 20 minutes in the icy water – courage that was to be recognised by a George Medal and a British Empire Medal.

However, the charge continued and in the ensuing fracas the attackers took three genuine casualties – a broken arm, a broken leg and one man knocked unconscious by a blow from a lead-filled cosh wielded by one of my blokes. I admit that I was responsible for parrying a thrust from a Canadian and heaving him across the emergency water main then running along the promenade – he missed his footing and broke a leg.

The Umpire (joyful at the sight of such a fracas on a black night) awarded the 'battle' to us and had the Canadians withdraw. On Sunday, we got down to the real business of the weekend – the Canadian assault on the town perimeter which, again, was awarded to the Home Guard.'

The War Diary does not record what the locals felt about the battle which raged across the Borough that weekend. However, on 25 June, the QOR received a visit from the Eastbourne Police in connection with damage to property. There was a second complaint two days later, but the diarist is unsympathetic:

'The police telephoned in connection with the property damaged in Eastbourne during street fighting practice with the 21 Sussex HG. Live ammunition and in some cases grenades were used in a street of houses ruined by air raids [Bourne Street]. *The HG denied all knowledge of this damage. It is to be hoped that the period of training which ended with mutual goodwill will not be spoiled by such a trivial damage claim on a property already damaged by the enemy. The property owner claimed that felt covering his already bomb-shattered windows had been torn off, a window frame broken, a door panel knocked out and two rows of onions in his garden trodden down. The damage he assessed at £20. The gentleman would seem to be an opportunist!'*

The 'Battle Drill' mentioned by George Humphrey above refers to a particularly tough training regime – one initially crusaded among Canadian forces by the Calgaries at the time of their detachment to Eastbourne in the winter of 1941/2.

As part of the hardening up process, men were made to visit local slaughterhouses and watch animals killed; they were sent to hospitals to see operations in progress. Speed marches in battle kit were held daily, and the training included cliff scaling while live rounds were fired overhead. Men were put into trenches and over-run by tanks. Thousands and thousands of live rounds were used in field-firing practices – never had Canadian forces had such an opportunity to become proficient with their weapons except in actual combat.[52]

17
Don't you know there's a war on?

With the notable exception of Operation Jubilee, the raid against Dieppe, the Canadian army in the UK did not engage in ground combat in the European theatre until the invasion of Sicily in July 1943.[*] However, Canadians obviously shared the same risks as civilians when it came to air raids. In the UK they suffered 420 casualties from air raids, of which 120 were fatal.[53]

The Edmontons, part of the 2nd Infantry Brigade of the Canadian 1st Division along with the PPCLI and the Seaforths, arrived here during the afternoon of 9 August 1942, having marched from Shoreham via Bishopstone in two days. Their BHQ was Prideaux Place, a house which had been the BHQ of the Calgaries in December 1941 and would fill this function again for the Hastings and Prince Edward Regiment in February 1943.

Again, a War Diary praises the quality of accommodation in and around Prideaux Road: 'The homes in this area are exceptionally well situated, though we must confess there are very few inhabitants left in this town.' On 10 August, it records that the Edmontons immediately set about digging slit trenches behind each of their billets: 'As we expect some air raids in this district.' And how right they were! The following day we read:

'Digging proceeds. The ground here is chalky and makes it a tricky job. At about 2305 hours, we had a real air raid. B Company [HQ at 8 Carew Road] *and C Company HQ* [Merrivale, Ashburnham Road] *were busy putting out incendiaries in the vicinity of their billets as well as removing furniture from civilian homes.* [A Company HQ at Manaos, 40 Kings Drive, HQ Company at 30 Carew Road

---

[*]However, two men of Norwegian descent with The Saskatoon Light Infantry were attached to the expeditionary force at Narvik in 1940 as interpreters. These were perhaps the first men of the Canadian Army to see action during WW2.

and the Regimental Aid Post at Dodleston, 14 Ashburnham Road.] *Several fires started in vicinity of railway station. One high explosive and several incendiaries in our transport park destroying three 30cwt trucks and one 13cwt truck.'*

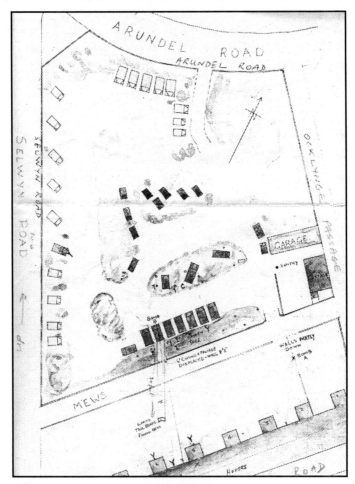

A new type of incendiary with an explosive head fell among trucks of the Edmontons in the orchard of Glenthorne, now Richmond Place. Fragments are marked 'Y' and blast is indicated 'X' in the report by the Ministry of Home Security. A sentry was blown off his feet by the explosion.

In fact, the damage was somewhat worse, as revealed in a report by experts sent to investigate what appeared to have been a new type of incendiary bomb with an explosive head. According to their findings, 40 lorries had been dispersed among trees and covered with nets in the orchard of what had been Glenthorne in Arundel Road.[*] Two of the bombs fell in the vicinity – one behind 25 Enys Road, in the lane between Selwyn Road and Ocklynge Lane, and the other where 9 Richmond Place stands today. Four lorries were destroyed, four were damaged beyond repair and 15 were slightly damaged. A sentry by the garage cottage in Ocklynge Lane was blown off his feet, and the rear of the houses in Enys Road sustained blast damage.[54]

It had been a true baptism of fire for the 'Eddies'.[†] In *Wartime Eastbourne,* George Humphrey comments:

> *'A number of questions arose over this particular raid: the sheer weight of the attack; its principal target area; the use of flares to ensure it got home in the right location; and the date. It came just prior to the ill-fated Dieppe raid about which so much controversy has raged over a suggested intelligence leak – this was not only the most severe night raid on the town but there was a deliberate intention to saturate a particular area.'*

The Edmontons were not the only ones to receive the attention of the Luftwaffe that night. Arthur Thorpe was a Wireless Operator with The Royal Canadian Corps of Signals, attached to the Canadian 2nd LAA Regiment [2 LAA]:

---

[*]Glenthorne in Arundel Road had been demolished to make way for flats, but the scheme was never realised - Eastbourne Civic Society Newsletter - Spring 1995.
[†]On 5 Nov 1942 the Luftwaffe was more kindly disposed towards the Edmontons. A Ju-88 flew over men at Folkington: 'So low that the pilot and crew were clearly visible and could be seen waving at us.'

'We had moved from Worthing, and on the first night in our new billets we had an air raid which was mostly incendiary. We lived in a large house [Trevin Towers in Gaudick Road, now part of Brighton University] *enclosed by a high wall with a circular driveway and an elongated porch where it was convenient to alight from a car and for someone on guard duty. Several bombs struck the house and one came down through the eaves and almost hit the sentry. Bombs landed in the courtyard and our house was on fire with a good blaze. The fire department came but had considerable delay with the hydro-pump, but eventually the blaze was put out. The aircraft that hit our house was so low our aerial was knocked down.'*

However, the guns of 2 LAA fired back. The Regimental History states: '2 (Yorkton) Battery engaged the planes by the light of their own flares and fired 224 rounds, destroying one aircraft.' However, this achievement is not confirmed in CMHQ 106, the report dealing with Canadian AA successes.

Although the Edmontons and 2 LAA suffered material damage, they had no fatal casualties in this raid. Sadly this was not the case for A Company of 9th Canadian Field Ambulance, RCAMC, who were quartered at what had been Roborough next to the Princess Alice Hospital. Their trench shelter in the grounds of the former preparatory school received the full force of a bomb. The Diary reports that eight medics were killed outright, and a further three seriously injured. All were buried at Brookwood Cemetery.

Yet another bomb – probably from the same stick – landed in the front garden of 11 Upper Avenue, causing damage which is still visible to this day. George Humphrey recalls: 'A tree took a direct hit on the top of its trunk from a 250kg bomb and was hacked down to a tall stump with a splintered top. This tree still survives and, in summer leaf, shows no sign of having suffered in any way; only in winter can any indications be seen as to which tree it is.'

The assistance of the Edmontons during the raid on 11 August 1942 was greatly appreciated, and prompted the following letter from the Mayor, Alderman Rush:

> *I have received an account of the splendid work done on the night of 11-12th August by the members of your Regiment. I am writing as Mayor to express, on behalf of the citizens of Eastbourne, our sincere thanks for the real assistance given and for the risks cheerfully taken, which mean so much in these tragic incidents.*
>
> *Will you please convey to all ranks who took part in this splendid work the sincere thanks of the citizens of Eastbourne.*

It seems likely that the movement of the 2nd Canadian Infantry Brigade into Eastbourne on 9 August 1942 had triggered the night raid. In any event there followed a belated crackdown on security – and the stable door was firmly bolted. The War Diary of 2 LAA records that courts martial were held on 3, 4, 5 and 6 September and that two troopers were found guilty of disclosing the locations of certain military units to undercover officers. Both men were sentenced to two years' imprisonment. Security was put further to the test at the end of September when:

> *'Other intelligence men entered the lines of The Princess Patricia's Canadian Light Infantry.* [This unit was near Willingdon Roundabout and in Hampden Park along Glynde and Brassey Avenues and Brand Road.] *The intelligence men were dressed in German uniforms and claimed to be fire-watchers! Three companies accepted them before they were arrested by men of C Company. Later a bogus officer claiming to be a member of the Free French crossed the lines asking questions, but was not apprehended.'*[55]

The purge on security and the recent courts martial led to sleepless nights for HQ staff of the Edmontons. The War Diary on 7 October 1942 reports that papers relating to the recent change of command had been mislaid. The Adjutant believed that another officer had them, but this could not be confirmed because the latter was on a 48-hour pass: 'It is to be hoped that the Quartermaster has the papers for we dare not think what might happen if they are lost.' The wretched Adjutant, having discovered that the missing documents were not with the Quartermaster after all, then asked the Sanitary Men, who were also responsible for salvage:

> 'To his shock and surprise he found they remembered having sorted the papers out of an ash-bin and sending them on to the collection point. Frantic as an expectant father, the Adjutant rushed to the collection point, but the salvage had been sent to the paper mill at Newhaven. It was now a race against time, would the papers be re-pulped before he reached the mill? The Captain had 150 sacks to look through, but not without success. Oh, no, he retrieved all the documents alright but he'll never retrieve all the hair he pulled out of his head during the episode.'

A security scare had also occurred in February of the same year, when the Black Watch received on loan a couple of German uniforms to familiarise men with the appearance of the enemy:

> 'Worn by our Intelligence Platoon, these uniforms gave the troops a fairly accurate picture of what their opponents are going to look like when we do meet them in battle. The 'German soldier' must have been pretty true to form for, when he was being taken up to C Company in the Intelligence truck, a much-disturbed police constable phoned through to the Intelligence Officer with the report that he had seen a Nazi trooper in one of your trucks, and what should he do about it?'

Danger could appear from the sea. On 13 December 1942, the Edmontons record:

> 'Sometime before noon, a sea mine was sighted drifting in towards Eastbourne Pier. The local police took charge,

establishing it as being one of our own, tied it to the pier and declared that it could do no damage as these mines had a safety device that prevented them from exploding should they break loose. At 1600 hours approximately, for want of a safety device, the mine exploded, causing considerable damage to the pier and the hotels in the area. The local police were most surprised that it exploded and finally came to the conclusion that they had misidentified it, and that the mine was definitely a product of the enemy.'

On 18 December 1942, the run-up to Christmas saw a daylight attack by a Dornier 217 which dropped four large bombs at the junction of Terminus and Langney Roads. This raid is described by the Edmontons: 'Another sneak raider dropped bombs in Eastbourne today, this time in the business section. As usual the raider came over just at noon and caught innumerable Xmas shoppers. Up to now it is definitely known that there are 8 dead with many more injured and still buried under the debris.' The final count was 18 dead and 37 injured; Canadian troops assisted the civil authorities at the scene. At the time of writing, the diarist probably did not know that fellow Canadians had narrowly escaped death during this raid. A Light Aid Detachment of The Royal Canadian Ordnance Corps was based in Tideswell Road, behind Marks and Spencer. Their location was probably in former stables, which had by then been converted into garages.

It is interesting to conjecture about intelligence, and whether pilots had been allocated targets for the raid on 7 March 1943. At lunchtime that Sunday, a force of 18 Fw-190[56] fighter-bombers swooped on the town from the Downs. Some of their bombs struck Meads, where elements of 2 Fd Regt were billeted. One bomb passed through the roof of 9–11 Meads Street before exploding in front of what had been St Augustine's School at the corner of Milnthorpe and Chesterfield Roads. This was almost certainly a 2 Fd Regt billet, but luckily the troops were away on an exercise. The same bomb also damaged other likely billets – 12, 14 and 16 Milnthorpe Road. Writing at Firle Park, the diarist states on 8

105

March 1943: '12 Fw-190s raided Eastbourne, destroyed 2nd Cdn Field Regiment Sergeants' Mess and 7 Battery HQ House, damaged 7 Battery billets.' The following day it is noted: 'Work party to Eastbourne to clean up billets damaged in air raid.'

The raiders also hit RAF quarters – the Mostyn Hotel, which stood on the seafront where Grand Court is today. The hotel accommodated WAAFs, probably attending a course in aircraft recognition, and there were five service casualties. A second plane aimed a 500kg bomb at an RAF pylon at the top of Warren Hill and scored a direct hit, blowing the pylon high into the air.[57]

The author was on the receiving end of this raid. I had been invited to lunch with my grandparents and an uncle on leave at 28 Meads Street, but was late because of a broken spring in a clockwork train. My grandmother [Clara Mackay] came to fetch me at 32 Meads Street and arrived just as the bomb exploded at number 28. But for the broken spring, we would probably have been killed along with my grandfather [Glendale Mackay]. My uncle [S D Mackay] was trapped under the debris but crawled free. It was therefore fascinating 60 years later to discover the translation of an interview which was broadcast the following day on the German Home Service.[58] The report refers to the raid on Eastbourne and correlates with what took place on the ground.

> **German Home Service at 9.20 pm on 8 March 1943**
>
> **Reporter**: *When you started at midday today, Hauptmann, we saw a number of aircraft each carrying a heavy bomb and knew the town in Southern England, which was your target, would have to pay heavily for the terror attacks on German civilians. But we also knew that yours would be no easy task. A clear blue sky stretched across the Channel, depriving you of cloud cover.*

Hauptmann: It wasn't as bad as it sounds. Even if someone on the cliffs sees or hears us coming, we have left him far behind before he can raise the alarm.

Reporter: So you were over the town at 13.00. What was it like to have the whole formation flying behind you?

Hauptmann: During the approach, all you see is water and aircraft. I led the attack and saw relatively little of the result. The others will be able to tell you more.

Reporter: Leutnant, you dropped your bomb immediately after the Hauptmann.

Leutnant: I saw him drop his bomb on a military camp to my right. I was concentrating on the town, but when I saw that bomb, I thought the camp would do as well. Then I suddenly saw an AA gun firing at me and behind it a radio mast, surrounded by hutments and another AA gun. I climbed and released my bomb. I tried to see what had happened, but everything was obscured by an enormous cloud of smoke. I couldn't make out whether I had hit the mast or not.

Reporter: And you, Leutnant, were flying behind the [other] Leutnant and saw the result.

Leutnant: Yes, the bomb fell rather short, then bounced and exploded close to the base of the radio mast. When the cloud disappeared I saw that the mast had snapped and that the hutments had simply disappeared. This was confirmed to me by other aircraft.

Leutnant: We were making for the town when I saw the Rottenflieger [Flight Leader] climb and then dive down on a large block of buildings and release his bomb, which entered the first floor. The whole building seemed to disintegrate into a cloud of blue-black smoke.

The Leutnant refers to 'a large block of buildings' as the aircraft were making for the town. This must surely have been the parade of shops and maisonettes between 24 and 34 Meads Street. Then as today, with their expanse of black slate roof in contrast to the red tiles all around, they attract attention from the Downs.

A picture taken at St Omer Wizernes near Calais in the spring of 1942 showing a Fw-190 of *Stab* JG 26. Fighter-bombers such as this were responsible for most of the Tip and Run Raids against southern England between May 1942 and June 1943.

The Luftwaffe units which launched the raid were 10/JG 2 and 10/JG 54.[59] The German news report would have been filed as the aircraft returned to Caen and St Omer Wizernes respectively.

18
Coming in for Flak

It must be said that by 1943 most of Eastbourne's Canucks would have felt a growing sense of frustration. Here they were, armed to the teeth with the latest military hardware, and in tip-top physical condition after endless runs in full kit over the Downs. They had volunteered for active service overseas, and now wanted part of the action. Yet every time the enemy appeared, it was from the air and all they could do was crouch in a trench and hope his bombs, cannon shells and machine-gun bullets would land elsewhere.

Both sides were equipped with fine AA guns – British and Canadian LAA units had the 40mm Bofors as seen above. The German 88mm Flak gun was dual-purpose in that it also served as an anti-tank weapon. The Bofors was occasionally used in a ground role, especially in North Africa.

However, there was one group of men who did have the satisfaction of hitting back at the enemy – the Light Anti-Aircraft crews with their Bofors guns. And raiders did indeed come in for plenty of Flak – even though this was not always as effective as the gunners would have hoped.

Developed in Sweden and manufactured under licence in Britain, the 40mm Bofors was a formidable weapon capable of firing armour-piercing or high explosive shells to an effective ceiling of 5,000 feet.[60] The gun had a crew of five or six, and was easily towed behind a standard army lorry. However, the gunners had little protection, and were vulnerable if attacked head-on by a fighter-bomber flying low and fast. In the event of a head-to-head duel between a diving Fw-190 and a Bofors, the odds would have been heavily on the aircraft.

Richard Wittmann during pilot training in Austria in 1940. His Fw-190 was damaged over Eastbourne by Canadian AA fire.

In Hanover in August 2004, the author interviewed a former Fw-190 pilot, Richard Wittmann. His father had served in the regular army during the Great War; his brother was reported missing at Stalingrad. When Wittmann volunteered for the Luftwaffe in October 1939, he was already an experienced glider pilot. An Obergefreiter [Senior Aircraftman – an aircrew rank in the Luftwaffe], he was 'the one that got away' when Eastbourne's power station at Roselands was devastated on 26 August 1942 during a raid by two Fw-190s of 10/JG26 which were based at St Omer Wizernes, near Calais. The Flight Leader, Oberfeldwebel [Master Pilot] Werner Kassa, piloting the other aircraft was brought down on Lottbridge Drove. This success was claimed by a Bren gunner of the Seaforths of Canada on the roof of Caffyns Garage, near the present Seaside Roundabout.[61]

A number of Bofors of 2 LAA also engaged Wittmann as he escaped. Optimistic claims are made in the Diary: 'Number 2 Battery, brought down one in the Channel by Bofors fire.' And from behind the present Leisure Pool: 'Bofors of A Troop, 2nd (Yorkton) LAA Battery [in September 1940, the first Canadian LAA unit to have arrived in the UK] expended five rounds and claimed one hit.' From the Holywell gun position,[*] a Bofors of 'K' Troop, 54th LAA Battery, engaged the Fw-190: 'One fighter-bomber fired at when receding over town at 500 feet. Two rounds fired – nothing claimed as aircraft was at extreme range.' While conceding that the Seaforths had indeed downed the first aircraft with machine-gun fire, the Diary of 2 LAA unit states:

'The other plane was engaged by one of our guns, and a direct hit observed on the tail. It was seen to waver several times with smoke and flames pouring from it as it flew out to sea. The above is also confirmed by the Coastguard at Eastbourne. Reports since indicate that it crashed in the Channel.'

The War Diary of the Seaforths reports not only two kills, but also a considerable PR success:

'All credit to Sergeant N C Forsbeck and his anti-aircraft platoon, they shot down two of Germany's prized Focke Wulf 190s, which raided Eastbourne at 0851hrs this morning. The first crashed into a ditch near the gasometers. The second is believed to have crashed several miles out to sea. The locals who, up to the present have been rather cool and distant to us, as most southern English folk are, livened

---

[*]Vestiges of this site can be seen on the path from the Foot of Beachy Head – map reference 598970

up considerably, and free drinks were the order in neighbouring pubs.'

However, despite the Seaforths' claim that they had downed, two planes, there is little doubt that Witmann's aircraft was hit by a Bofors and not a Bren. When he landed, his tail plane was found to have a hole some 40mm in diameter. There was other damage, but he made it home thanks to the aircraft's self-sealing fuel tanks. When interviewed in Hanover in August 2004, he was intrigued to see photographs from the *Eastbourne Chronicle* of the wrecked generating plant. The damage was so severe that the pictures were initially censored. He had not seen his comrade brought down.

This shot of the wrecked power station at Roselands after the raid by two Fw-190s on 26 August 1942 was not released until a year later.

As far as intelligence is concerned, although the Luftwaffe must have known that hotels and large houses in Eastbourne were quarters for troops, Wittmann cannot recall being allocated targets: 'We were over the towns for only a few minutes and would seek out targets of opportunity such as railway stations and public utilities.'

Yet fighter-bombers struck the Cavendish on 4 May 1942, and the Mostyn on 7 March 1943 – both were accommodation for RAF personnel.[62] On Hastings seafront, Marine Court was hit on 24 September 1942 when it housed aircrew cadets,[63] as was the Albany Hotel on 23 May 1943. In the latter incident several Canadian soldiers were killed.[64]

Another hitherto unpublished photograph by Bob Hurst of Toronto. The east wing of the Cavendish Hotel was destroyed on 4 May 1942. There were four service casualties in the Orderly Room, where the Coronet Bar is now situated. Casualties would have been heavier but for a compulsory sports afternoon.

Richard Wittmann was with 10/JG26 from 7 July to 30 November 1942. The engagement on 26 August 1942 was not the first time he had been in action against Canadians. A few days earlier he had flown over Dieppe against Operation Jubilee.

Richard Wittmann after a crash landing in 1943. He was 'the one who got away' when Eastbourne's power station was hit on 26 August 1942 – the other aircraft was shot down at Lottbridge Drove. The pilot, Oberfeldwebel Kassa, was buried at Langney, but later exhumed and taken to the German War Cemetery at Cannock Chase. Parts of Kassa's aircraft were unearthed when the Drove was being widened in 1963.

He destroyed his logbook in May 1945 but recalls a mission in the Brighton area [probably Littlehampton on 30 July 1942], another against Newhaven [probably 1 August 1942] and against Deal [16 October 1942]. However, the heaviest raid in which he took part was against Canterbury on 31 October 1942 when 52 - 62 fighter-bombers from three units caused 29 fatal casualties, with a further 53 detained in hospital. There was widespread damage, which once again included an electricity generating works.[65]

Towards the end of the war, Richard Wittmann was sent to the Eastern Front, but was injured and pronounced unfit for flying after his Fw-190 crash-landed in April 1945. His unit withdrew to a point near the Danish border where he was taken prisoner by the British. He was released from captivity on 30 July 1945, and arrived home four days later to find his parents alive but the family house in ruins.

Unteroffizier Alfred Immervoll – shot down into the sea off Beachy Head by Canadian fire on 23 January 1943.

One of the Fw-190s flying with Wittmann against Canterbury on 31 October 1942 lost part of a wing when it hit a balloon cable. Interestingly, the pilot of this aircraft, Unteroffizier [Sergeant] Alfred Immervoll, was himself shot down on 23 January 1943 off Whitbread Hollow by Canadians. The success was attributed to a Bofors AA gun of 2 LAA although the PPCLI shared the credit.[66] At the time, the PPCLI were based at Rottingdean, but men were sent to Beachy Head on a daily basis.

The aircraft were Fw-190s [one mistaken for a Me-109 by the Canadians] returning to France. They had been ordered to attack Hailsham, but had hit Polegate before machine-gunning the Old Town and Meads districts of Eastbourne. The scrapbook kept by the author's father notes: 'Bullets knocked tiles off house next to ours in Meads Street.'

The Bofors belonged to 2nd (Yorkton) Battery of 2 LAA and was firing from a position [probably MR 595966] above Whitbread Hollow. When questioned after the incident, the NCO in charge of the gun, Sergeant A Horechka, stated: 'I gave the order to fire and several shots were fired and a direct hit was scored on the plane, which exploded and fell into the sea between 400 and 500 yards out and almost opposite the poultry farm.'[67] The farm stood immediately behind the present sports pavilion in Whitbread Hollow.

However, Carl Darrock, then a Private with the PPCLI, put the case for his own involvement when he and another soldier were manning a machine-gun post at Beachy Head. The Germans passed over their position, and when one of the aircraft saw the others being fired at, it dipped under a 25-foot cliff [probably Cow Gap] and headed straight towards them. Darrock and the other gunner, Private Jack Andros, opened up with their Brens. They felt they had killed the pilot as the plane veered and dived into the water. When the authorities came to investigate, all that was left was a patch of oil on the water. About six days later a body, subsequently identified as that of Unteroffizier Immervoll, was washed onto the beach. Darrock commented: 'We received a bit of money and a three-day pass to London for what we did.'[68]

Whether the fire originated from a Bofors or from Brens, by an extraordinary coincidence and unbeknown to them, the Canadians had just avenged the death of a comrade. A few moments earlier, one of the German aircraft had bombed Polegate, killing Gunner Stanley Gifford of The 8th Field Regiment, RCA, who happened to be on leave and staying with his wife's parents. Gunner Gifford was buried at Ocklynge Cemetery – his is the only Canadian grave of the Second World War in Eastbourne. There were two other fatal casualties, one of whom was the soldier's mother-in-law.

In addition to the Holywell and Whitbread Hollow sites, it is known that 2 LAA had a position down at the poultry farm itself, and another at Well Combe, above the allotments in Upper Dukes Drive. The War Diary also refers to a site on the Royal Eastbourne Golf Links, 300 metres south of Summerdown Road, and another on the Western Lawns by the Grand Hotel.

Number 35 Battery of the 1st LAA Regiment also operated in Eastbourne from September of the same year, with quarters at Downs House [now part of St Bede's School] in Dukes Drive.

Overall responsibility for AA was in the hands of ADGB (Air Defence Great Britain), and as LAA units arrived or were formed in the UK, they came under 1st Canadian Anti-Aircraft Brigade at Colchester for training and duty under Anti-Aircraft Command. Canadian batteries were deployed throughout the south of England, but also owed allegiance to their own brigades and trained with their 'parent' formations. As public pressure to counter Tip and Run Raids increased, so changes were introduced. One of these was Operation Duckshooting. The history of 2 LAA states:

'The Canadians contributed further to the AA defences of south coast towns when Operation Order 'Duckshooting' was initiated on 4 October 1942. Some 40 to 50 sites were chosen along the coast and were manned from time to time by one troop per battery so that extra sites were manned at all times. This scheme was also carried out by other Canadian AA Regiments, while static defences were manned by English AA Personnel.'

On 1 October, LAA crews were ordered to fire without recognition on any plane approaching from the water at under 500ft, although this was later amended to exclude flying boats. The news was greeted with enthusiasm: 'This is an order for which we have been waiting because it is practically impossible to recognise a fast, direct approach till it is too late.' While Duckshooting was in force, Canadian Bofors would move from position to position, never staying more than 48 hours in one place. Yet the new orders had a downside. On 26 October, 2 LAA notes ruefully: 'Eastbourne bombed; 4 houses demolished; 6 dead, 20 injured. None of our guns fired as all away on Duckshooting'.

The author has heard that at times the Canadians committed one third of their LAA in Britain to our air defence. Although AA

Command welcomed the extra firepower, RAF pilots were less happy as guns would open fire from unexpected places.

Some 52 sites, British (static) and Canadian (mobile), were earmarked for Duckshooting in the Eastbourne area; many out of town, but also several in what are now housing and industrial estates. However, the mobile sites were not necessarily permanent and some may not have been used at all. [See Appendix B.]

Despite the dangers of war, the Downs remained an irresistible adventure playground for local boys. To conclude this chapter about LAA sites, here is a curious link with the past recalled by a former pupil of Downsmead School, Michael Paine:

During the summer of 1943 I was with some friends in Paradise Wood. Aged thirteen, I was the youngest. We walked to the disused reservoir, which, in those days, was uncovered: the bottom, some 60 feet down, was littered with rubbish. There was a pipe running down one side and we clambered down to explore. After we had fooled around for a while, my friends climbed back up. Being the youngest and the smallest, I could get only half-way up, when I simply slid back down again. My friends got help from some Canadians at a Bofors site on the hill. Some of the men came back with a rope and hauled me to safety.

Ten years later, I was working for the Toronto Hydro Electric System and would sit playing chess with the dispatcher waiting for jobs to come in. One night, he told me he had been billeted in Polegate and knew Eastbourne well. We were talking about the town when he suddenly said, 'Do you know, I was up on the hill one day and pulled a kid out of a pit.' Imagine my surprise – and his – when I told him the kid had been me! I only remember that his first name was Burt, but I shall never forget his smiling face peering over the edge of the reservoir, and his strong grip as he pulled me out. [For details of this unit and gun site, see Endnote.][69]

19
Operation Jubilee

No Canadian forces then based in Eastbourne took part in Operation Jubilee, the raid against Dieppe on 19 August 1942, although there are reports that some were at the Redoubt before the raid,[70] and so it is possible that the fortress was used as an assembly point before the embarkation at Newhaven. The situation was followed closely as news of the operation started to break. Unaware of the disaster unfolding across the Channel, the Edmontons' Diary is initially upbeat: 'Great news is received at noon that the 4th and 6th Brigades plus The Calgary Tank Regiment are in action at Dieppe on the coast of France.' One hour later: 'Four patrols of 15 men each are to be sent along the beaches in this area to pick up stray barges on their return from the raid. Three officers were sent to Newhaven at 1700 hours to help entrain the wounded on their return.' The upbeat tone continues: 'Naturally we are jealous, but as the names of those chosen were chosen from a hat we were just unlucky.'* The diarist of the Seaforths writing at Pevensey is initially even more optimistic:

> 'Great numbers of aircraft of all description had been flying back and forth across the Channel making it quite clear to everyone that "something" was going on. Newspaper reports and news commentators on the radio had told of a big raid on Dieppe, just opposite us on the French coast. The 4th and 6th Brigades of the 2nd Canadian Division, accompanied by the 3rd and 4th Commandos, and detachments from other arms of the Canadian forces had landed and were proceeding to thoroughly wipe out important points in and around the town. Supported by the

---

*Or lucky – for Operation Jubilee incurred heavy losses. C P Stacey in *Six Years of War* states that of a force of some 5,000 Canadians, there were 3,367 casualties, of which 907 were fatal. 1946 Canadian officers and men were captured; at least 568 of these were wounded.

RAF and the RN they made a good job of it – rumours especially are flying high.'

LAA units from Eastbourne were committed during the evacuation phase: 'To provide additional cover for the returning troops, Number 2 Battery [HQ Westbrook, Gaudick Rd] and Number 54 Battery [HQ the Moorings, St John's Rd] of 2 LAA were sent to Newhaven.' On 5 September, in an attempt to demoralise Canadian troops, a German aircraft dropped leaflets on the town showing the aftermath. However, the impact was minimal because the canister landed intact on the roof of the Luxor Cinema [Pevensey Road] and only a few leaflets reached soldiers or civilians. The Edmontons' War Diary comments:

'German propagandists have drawn up a pictorial leaflet of the aftermath of Dieppe and intended to distribute them in this area. However, the container, after being dropped from a plane did not explode, and fell to the earth intact. Several of these leaflets have been received by the unit and depict derelict equipment, prisoners etc, captured by the Hun. All in all it is a remarkable piece of propaganda.'

German commando-style raids against the Sussex coast had been on the cards since the fall of France – in the wake of Operation Jubilee the risk increased. However, there had previously been a number of false alarms. The Diary of the Maisonneuves has an entry for 24 November 1941:

'There was a brief alert during the night in the sector of Company D. At 2230hrs two men on patrol noticed signal flares which seemed to indicate that someone was in distress. These were followed shortly afterwards by what appeared to be a light flashing in Morse code. The beach lights were at once switched on revealing two landing craft heading for the shore. All the men took up 'Action Stations' and prepared for any eventuality. However, instructions were given that no one should open fire until orders were received from an officer.

Just then an officer in charge of beach lights advised Captain Charlebois that they were English landing craft. Having first ascertained that this was indeed the case, Captain Charlebois nevertheless kept his men at the ready. When the craft came within hailing distance, one of the soldiers on board called out: "Where the hell are we?" He had been mystified for a moment by the exchanges in French between our men on the beach. It turned out that they were a group of Commandos returning from a raid in France and had lost their way. As they came ashore, the landing craft were damaged on some of our anti-invasion defences. The officers from the raid were put up in D Company's mess and told us what they could about the raid. One of their men had been injured by a machine-gun bullet on the beach in France. Our visitors stayed with us for two days before being transported back to base.'

The Black Watch, also part of the 5th Canadian Infantry Brigade, comment on the incident in their own Diary written at Willingdon: 'It was a good lesson to the shore troops to find how close these assault landing craft may come before they can be detected.' However, less than ten days later, the Diary reports a relaxation:

'The Battalion observation post which hitherto has been manned 24 hours a day by personnel of the Intelligence section from their locality on the edge of Beehive Plantation [top of Butts Lane] *was today vacated in accordance with the new policy now in effect that guards, patrols etc should be reduced to an absolute minimum. It is felt that our present air supremacy and the absence of any imminent danger from enemy attack warrants this reduction.'*

Measures to repel invaders were originally known as Operation Afloat, but were later changed to Bugbear, probably because it was feared the security of the former had been compromised. The Diary of the Black Watch notes on 4 February 1942:

121

'This evening, at 1955hrs, there took place the first real "Afloat". The real or suspected danger came from the direction of Brighton; the only thing observed by troops in this area were flares from the west. Our A Company, as duty company, turned out and carried out their tasks with much confusion, but it was apparent that certain other sub-units and civilian organizations either had not been properly informed of the plan of action or else have never given much thought to what part they should play. The excitement was short-lived: nothing happened and "Stand Down" was ordered at 2115hrs.'

At Pevensey Bay, the situation was tenser for the Maisonneuves: 'The Battalion was put on stand-by and in C Company's sector, shadowy figures were believed to have been seen on the shore. Several shots were fired and, at the same time, flares were seen over the Channel. Brigade was informed and "Afloat" was ordered. Two hours later, as nothing had happened and everything was quiet, we all went home.'

On the night of 3 April 1942, another invasion scare is reported in the Diary of the Black Watch:

'Last night at approximately 2000hrs the Brigade Major phoned to say that a raid by sea-borne and/or airborne troops was expected on the RAF [Radar] *station at Pevensey. The carrier platoon was ordered to stand to and the duty coy, also. At last it looked as though something might happen. Shortly after midnight the alert went but the all clear sounded some minutes later. And so the night went – no paratroops, no seaborne troops, no enemy, and NO SLEEP! Stand down came from Brigade at 0726hrs.'*

The next day, the Acting General Officer Commanding Canadian 2nd Division announced that a raid was expected in this area on 5 or 6 April. This information was to be passed to all ranks and anti-raid precautions rehearsed and checked. His closing words are reported by the Black Watch: 'This is a God-sent chance for the Division to get into action and give the troops a lift in morale.' The information, he said, had come from the RAF and a parachute battalion was in France, ready to come over.

The likelihood of German raids increased with Dieppe, and minds were focussed by the prospect of retaliatory strikes. An Anti Raid Instruction was circulated on 11 August 1942, and later amended in a Plan to Defeat Invasion by the 2nd Canadian Infantry Brigade at its HQ at Westlords in Willingdon Road on 8 September 1942.

Westlords, at the junction of Park Lane and Willingdon Road, was HQ of the 2nd Canadian Infantry Brigade in August 1942, the time of the Dieppe raid. Retaliatory action was anticipated in the Eastbourne area and the Brigade drafted a Plan to Defeat Invasion at this house.

The orders from 2nd Brigade HQ are comprehensive and wide-ranging – details below are limited to the Eastbourne area. Upon receipt of the code word Bugbear the following movements were to be initiated.

The PPCLI would proceed from its quarters in Willingdon and Hampden Park to the airfield at Friston and to Birling Gap; the Seaforths would move from Hankham to defend the RAF radar station at Pevensey, and the Edmontons would move from Upperton to take responsibility for the Beachy Head sector. An alternative responsibility was earmarked for the anti-tank components of the PPCLI and the Edmontons, who would cover the beach from Eastbourne to Cooden. All military petrol pumps in the area would be immobilised; a list of all civilian pumps was held at Eastbourne Police Station – these would also be immobilised in liaison with Brigade.

The 2nd Canadian Infantry Brigade HQ refined its Anti Invasion Precautions on 7 October 1942, reiterating a list of danger points where sea-borne raiding parties could be expected: (a) underneath the cliffs on either side of Birling Gap (b) Eastbourne Pier to Langney Point (c) Pevensey Bay from Langney Point to Cooden. Landings by paratroops were considered possible at: (a) the Downs west of a line Eastbourne – Polegate (b) strip of beach known as Crumbles (c) Pevensey Levels (possible but hazardous). Glider landings were envisaged: (a) in the Crapham Down – Bullock Down area, north and north-west of Beachy Head (b) on the Crumbles and the stretch of paved road between Pevensey and the Lamb public house at Hooe. Enemy aircraft might attempt landings at: (a) Friston Aerodrome and (b) on the road between Pevensey and the Lamb at Hooe.

The increased state of alert along the coast following the Dieppe raid meant that stand-to companies were confined to billets from one hour before sunset to one hour after sunrise daily; men were permitted to sleep, but at ten minutes' notice. These companies carried a minimum of equipment to include personal weapons, bayonets and 50 rounds of ammunition per man.

59 Park Avenue – Then and Now
Typical of houses in Willingdon and Hampden Park occupied by
Canadians who would counter German retaliatory raids – wartime picture
by Bob Hurst of Toronto in 1942. The movement of regiments around the
country was a complex logistical exercise. Accommodation would be
vacated by one unit in the morning and taken over by another in the
afternoon. For example in Willingdon and Hampden Park, the Seaforths
were replaced by The Royal Canadian Regiment [RCR] on 12 April 1943.
The RCR had its BHQ and HQ Company at Malaya House in Park Lane.
Its A and Support Companies were in Brassey Avenue and Brand Road,
with B Company at Changla in Park Avenue, near what is now
Chalvington Road, and C Company off the present Woodland Avenue in
the Coppice (MR 594019). Some two weeks later, on 29 April, the RCR left
for Inverary in Scotland after handing over to The Royal Winnipeg Rifles.

The PPCLI maintained bicycle patrols (three Bren guns, one
NCO and seven other ranks) at the junction of Beachy Head Road
and the road leading to the Head and East Dean, and another in the
vicinity of Birling Farm. The Seaforths mounted similar patrols:
one in the vicinity of Lottbridge Drove and the junction with
Seaside, and another at Rockhouse Bank. The Edmontons

provided two patrols: one at the sports pavilion in Princes Park, and the other in the vicinity of St Aubyn's Road and the seafront.

The Anti Raid Precautions also note that the 21st Sussex (Eastbourne) Battalion of the Home Guard was to maintain a daily in-lying picket at 11 Devonshire Place between 2100 hours and 0500 hours. In the event of an attack, the codeword Bugbear would send these men to assist in the defence of the coastal gun positions at the Wish Tower. The Home Guard patrolled Grand Parade and the stretch between the Bandstand and Penhale Road. George Humphrey recalls that two men also patrolled between the Wish Tower and the Foot of Beachy Head; two more between the Wish Tower and the Pier, and a further two between the Pier and the Fishing Station. Anything out of the ordinary was first to be reported to Canadian troops in the pill-boxes along the lower promenade and then by runner to the Home Guard Post at 11 Devonshire Place.

Even the RAF Equipment Training School based in seafront hotels and the sailors of HMS Marlborough at Eastbourne College were assigned a role. The RAF maintained a 24-hour patrol between Holywell Pumping Station and the Bandstand and, as weapons and trained personnel became available, they would be joined by ratings from HMS Marlborough.

20
Listening to the enemy

The vast majority of servicemen at Eastbourne would not see an enemy soldier until after the invasion – and then probably only those Germans who were already prisoners or who had been killed in action. Yet small units of The Royal Canadian Corps of Signals listened around the clock to the enemy 'talking' – albeit through the medium of Morse code. One unit of eavesdroppers consisted of men of Special Wireless Section (No. 1 SW Section Type B), who were in town from May to December 1943. For the first three months they operated from wireless vans on the Downs and were billeted at Frinton in Upper Carlisle Road.

Mr J G Adams, a Canadian who chose to stay in Britain after the war, had served with the RCCS:

'We had a short climb up behind the house on the other side of the road to our vans [towards Paradise Wood]. *From there we had a grand view of the town and it was a favourite spot for the German low-flying fighters to let off a few rounds as they turned to cross the Channel again. We had some frights, but were very fortunate that none of our chaps were hit. Some of the men had been amateur radio operators – 'hams' as they were called – before the war; others (like me) had trained to be commercial operators on ships, aircraft and at airports.*

After we had joined up, they soon found out about our background and we were shipped to Ottawa for special training in monitoring work. The traffic we picked up was in Morse – four or five-letter groups – and so the messages could not be understood. However, our messages, together with those of other units doing the same work, were dealt with by the Intelligence people. There was a section of them living with us whose job it was to attend to that side of the work. We operated 24 hours a day and a lot of the work was to do with the movement of enemy troops on the other side of the Channel. Sometimes we would listen to a control station for days, and his related stations would, for example, reply only on the hour with a short signal. Suddenly there might be a great deal of activity, which usually indicated that an army unit was on the move. Thus our work was just a small part of a greater network obtaining information from across the Channel. In August 1943, we moved to Chaseley, where we found that one of the rooms was completely decorated in a Japanese motif – how ironic that was!'

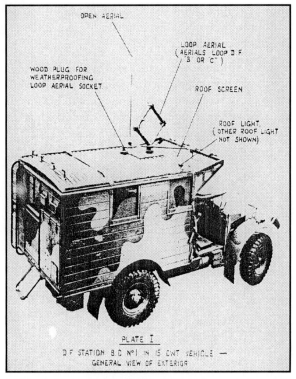

Signals van of the Canadian 'Spies of the Airwaves'. Reception was excellent above Paradise Wood, but the team was moved to Chaseley for fear the specialists might be wiped out by fighter-bombers.

The Special Wireless units combined both signallers (SW Section) and intelligence staff (WI Section) working together as a team. The SW Section had two Signals Officers and 76 men, including operators, drivers, dispatch riders, technicians, cooks, store men and an administration clerk.[71]

They were equipped with National HRO receivers for HF (short wave) work. They also had Hallicrafters S-27 receivers for VHF reception and DF (direction finding) sets. The WI Section comprised three Intelligence Officers, a Sergeant and 18 German linguists and analysts.[72]

The American 'National HRO' receiver was the mainstay of allied Y Services – the units eavesdropping on enemy military and diplomatic radio traffic. The removable 'drawer' is a coil pack – each receiver has several such packs which the operator would slot in and out to cover the entire short wave radio spectrum. Compared with other receivers of its day the HRO was very selective, thus enabling the operator to pick out weak Morse signals amid interference. HROs were purchased in large numbers from the USA, and continued in use after the war by licensed amateur radio operators, including at the author's station – G3MHF.

On Boxing Day 1943, the men were told to pack their personal kit. From Eastbourne they moved to a holding camp at Chobham.

There they received medication against malaria in preparation for deployment to Italy with the rest of 1st Canadian Corps. On 6 January 1944, they left by sea for action on the battlefield.[73]

However, this was not the only signals intelligence (Y-Service) unit to have served in the town. From 2 January to 26 March 1944, Number 2 Canadian Special Wireless Section Type B and its associated Wireless Intelligence Section were also at Chaseley.

A Canadian direction-finding trailer above Meads. The white gable of 'Holywell Priory' (see page 22) appears above the brow. From the Downs, intercept operators monitored radio traffic and took bearings on German Condor aircraft as they flew reconnaissance flights over the North Sea towards Iceland. They were trained to recognise the various 'fists' (Morse code sending styles) of individual enemy operators to help identification when the Germans changed call signs.

In March or April 1944, a British Royal Corps of Signals detachment (118 Special Wireless Unit) took over Chaseley and carried out similar intercept duties.

One of the British operators recalled that their receivers were also in the Japanese Room, and had memories of a sunken bath: 'A more dangerous way of getting oneself clean I cannot imagine!'[74]

21
Ubique

The Latin word 'Ubique' means 'everywhere', and is the motto of The Royal Canadian Artillery and of The Corps of Royal Canadian Engineers, both of which can indeed be found at every location where the army is in action. RCE units in the town included the 16th Field Company of the Canadian 3rd Division in mid-May 1942, and the 3rd Field Company of the Canadian 1st Division in February 1943.

Eric Wilkes was with the 7th Field Company, which were Divisional Troops under Headquarters 2nd Divisional Engineers:

'I arrived in the UK in the late summer of 1940, and was stationed at the Grange and Lynchmere Schools from July 1941 to May 1942, when we left for the Isle of Wight to train for the raid on Dieppe. Our responsibilities included the preparation of demolitions, minefields and beach defences in the area. Our Brigade HQ was at Upper Dicker in Michelham Priory. We built an underground HQ close to the Priory and an emergency landing strip on Beachy Head. Our Number 3 Platoon was in charge of the beach defences between Beachy Head and Rye Harbour.'

The construction work was hard graft, but the engineers were able to call upon help from infantrymen. The Black Watch were surely involved in the construction of the defences noted above. On 19 November 1941, their War Diary states: 'Lieutenant Buchanan and a fatigue party of approximately 30 are at present working on the repair of the steel scaffolding defences along the beach on the Régiment de Maisonneuve's front [Pevensey]. This is part of a scheme of work laid down for the checking of scaffolding along the entire Brigade Front; this Battalion's front is to be worked on later.'

Labouring continued in January the following year: 'We are still supplying personnel for working parties within the Brigade area. Scaffolding party on the beach, working party for the construction of a proper road to the Downs from Willingdon, and we shall soon have to supply a working party for the digging of a ditch for a water main at Brigade HQ.' The road would have been an extension of Butts Lane at Willingdon, one of the many 'Tank Roads' constructed on the Downs. A busy training ground stretched between Babylon and Willingdon Hill; Winston Churchill visited training there when the early Churchill tanks were being used.[75]

The crash of a Wellington named 'Gold Coast II' crewed by New Zealanders is recalled by Eric Wilkes. The aircraft came down between Langney Point and Pevensey. He does not mention whether his unit recovered the aircraft, but the Black Watch are more specific on 15 October 1941: 'At 0650hrs a Wellington bomber made a forced landing in our area, near Hampden Park. Miraculously no one was hurt. The plane had been in the air for eight hours. We immediately put a guard on the plane and the crew proceeded to Friston Aerodrome from where they left for their base.'

The Royal Canadian Engineers were present in the town on 3 February 1943, when two sappers were subsequently decorated with the George and British Empire Medals for acts of great heroism at Eastbourne Pier:

'A good deal of work was done by various detachments in connection with the arrangement of camouflage nets on the six amusement piers along the south coast, so as to enable flotillas of small craft (such as wooden assault landing craft), some 300 in all, to be concealed. The raising, lowering and maintenance of these nets took quite a lot of sapper labour. During the period of working on the piers, the Corps added another two decorations to its roll.

*On 3 February 1943, N N Hunt of the 3rd Field Company fell
into the sea, striking the girders with his head and body.*

**The George Medal was established on 24 September 1940
for acts of great bravery and was intended primarily for
civilians. Awards to the military were confined to actions
for which purely military honours were not normally
granted.**

He had fallen at a 30-foot gap in the pier, which could only be crossed by cableway that day because of the heavy seas running. Lieutenant E T Galway and then, shortly, Sapper J Lorraine of the 3rd Field Company dove into the water to support Hunt, who was seriously injured.

Unable to overcome the undertow, all three were drawn seawards. A boat was launched and fortunately both the victim of the accident and his would-be rescuers were recovered after spending some 20 minutes in the icy waters. Galway was awarded the George Medal, and Sapper Lorraine the British Empire Medal in reward for their chilly task.[76]

22
Home on the range

The destruction of Belle Tout lighthouse by Canadian artillery fire remains a sore point for local people, many of whom mistakenly believe that the tower itself was the target. In fact, the guns were firing at wooden silhouettes of tanks which ran along rails at the east of building. John Donne's caption to a picture in *Sussex County Magazine* expresses the sentiments of many: 'The photograph shows what is left of the old lighthouse, shattered from the shells of friendly guns. Had it been Hitler's bombs on a defended building I could have viewed the wreck with the feeling that at least the 'old lady' went down fighting; but the knowledge that this need never have happened sickens me.'[77] The former lighthouse had been bought in 1923 by Sir James Purves-Stewart, the distinguished neurologist, who converted it into a house, where he entertained a number of distinguished guests between the wars including King George V and Queen Mary, and the Lord Chief Justice.[78]

However, in spite of strong local feeling about the destruction of Belle Tout, the author must confess to particular admiration for the handful of men around Birling Gap who were responsible for the Beachy Head and Michel Dene Anti-Tank Ranges. The fog and confusion of war, albeit on friendly terrain and without the horror of direct combat, comes across in the Diary of this unit, which was perched on the Downs from January to July 1943. For the range party, no mascot, no tradition, no glory and no motto – although the latter could well have been, 'Doing our best under difficult circumstances'. Strafed by fighter-bombers; blamed by locals for damage to Belle Tout; knee-deep in mud churned up as tanks and self-propelled guns ploughed across the Downland; cursed by artillerymen when firing was halted because of a convoy in the Channel; and up to their elbows in grease as they struggled to unblock drains at the Children's Delight, the pre-war holiday home at Birling Gap which served as a cookhouse for visiting artillery regiments.

Five ranges came under the unit, the largest being the Belle Tout Range for 25-pounder guns which fired at moving targets on rails. Colin Huggett in *60 Years of Narrow Gauge – Drusillas Railway* states: 'In 1940 the 9.5-inch miniature railway from the tea rooms at Alfriston was removed, and the track and trucks reassembled across the valley by the Canadian Army and used for moving target practice.'[79] Some local people believe this to be the track which saw service at Belle Tout, but there is another suggestion that the Drusillas railway was sold during the war and later set up at Tinkers Park at Hadlow Down. In any event, a narrow-gauge railway was indeed used, with tracks laid across the road below Belle Tout from a point near Hodcombe behind the dew-pond. The tracks went up the hill to the west of the present car park and stopped just short of the tower. During the summer, a trace can still be seen on the hillside and a bump, especially noticeable in frost, marks the point where they crossed the road:

> *'It consisted of a light railway (constructed in the autumn of 1941) crossing the valley formed by two hills, on one of which stands the old lighthouse. The rails ran part of the way up this hill, finishing in a deep dugout. Inside this was an old car – minus tyres – and the back wheel was used to tow a life-sized target of a tank along the rails. Soon afterwards firing began, and by 1942 it was incessant from dawn to dusk, never stopping even on Sundays.*[80]

From the firing-point near Cornish Farm, conventional artillery, self-propelled Sexton guns and tanks shot at the targets from a distance of some 900 metres. Eddie Williams, the retired manager of Bullock Down, lived at the farm with his parents during the war, and confirms there was an observation post at Frost Hill from where firing was directed.

The Shooters Bottom Range for 2-pounder anti-tank guns ran roughly from east to west between the cliff and the road from Beachy Head to Birling Gap. There was also a range at Michel Dene for 6-pounder guns, and two others described as Dive

Bomber and Sub Calibre ranges. However, the location of the latter two ranges is at present unclear.

Troops of the **Westminster Regiment firing 2-pounder guns on the Shooters Bottom range near Beachy Head. The outline of Belle Tout Lighthouse is clearly visible on the horizon – also the white scar tracing the path of the targets which ran on rails at the side of the tower. Howitzers and 25-pounder self-propelled guns fired at moving targets from a point near Cornish Farm. Men of the range party were billeted at the Birling Gap Hotel and in Nissen huts nearby. The picture appears courtesy of the Canadian Department of National Defence.**

The War Diary of the range party states that firing began on 1 January 1943, [later than indicated by James Donne] although the official opening was not until 14 January.* Almost at once came a foretaste of the problems which would beset the CO, Captain Ray

*The War Diary of the QOR refers to firing on 'the new 2-pounder anti-tank range at Birling Gap' on 30 June 1942. The CBOE Downs Preservation Committee was pressed to release land to the west of Beachy Head for military training purposes on 1 December 1942 according to *A Municipal History of Eastbourne 1938-1974* by J C Aspden.

Manbert, and his men. Units would arrive unexpectedly – and then have to return without firing because procedures were not yet in place to warn shipping in the Channel. Artillery regiments sometimes travelled long distances with guns and equipment, only to find the range had been double-booked. The fault did not lie with the range party, but they would surely have borne the brunt of the gunners' irritation. The wooden targets offered considerable resistance to the wind and were constantly being blown over.

The 25-pounder field gun was the standard howitzer used by British and Canadian artillery regiments during the Second World War. With a crew of six, the gun could fire five shells per minute to a maximum range of some 12,000 metres. Picture courtesy Library and Archives of Canada.

The first reference to damage appears in the War Diary on 24 January: 'Two more right angle hits on Belle Tout Lighthouse.' And the following day: 'The score of hits on the Lighthouse has reached thirteen, one on the garage doors.' Just when it seemed the gunners had got their eye in, a note on 12 February records: 'Belle

Tout scarred to the tune of 18 hits to date. All accidents, of course.' There was another hit on 17 February and one more the next day, but after this the standard of gunnery had either improved or no more hits were logged.

The end of January had brought more problems for the harassed Captain: 'Bad storm approaching and wind rising. Targets blown off the track about a dozen times today.' The bad weather continued with wind reaching speeds of 77mph. The targets kept blowing over, and it was impossible to operate the 25-pounder and the 6-pounder ranges. When The Lake Superior Regiment (Motor) came on 1 February, having made a 100-mile trip by convoy, the wind was blowing at 45-50mph and firing was cancelled. The men were obliged to return to their unit without having fired a shot. A further problem was mud churned up by tanks and other heavy vehicles: 'The mud is getting worse – almost impassable.' The problem continued deep into February: 'Those damn tanks again! They sure tear up the ground. We have an awful time to keep them on the road, [presumably from Birling Farm to Cornish Farm] which was built on purpose for their use.' From time to time, a shell would sever the cable which pulled the target trolley, and firing was halted while the range party sent out men to splice it together.

On 6 February 1943, the top brass arrived for a Divisional Demonstration – no fewer than 48 officers of Brigadier rank and upwards. Despite bad weather and difficult conditions all went well, but the afternoon produced a gruesome find at the Gap: 'At 1700hrs a German sailor was washed up on the beach, and transported into town. No head and little in the way of underclothes.' Two days later things were looking better for a successful shoot, but this was not to be. Manbert writes: 'Weather good, but a mine was washed up below Belle Tout. Range closed down for 90 minutes. Navy rendered the mine safe – we're having a lot of bad luck.' On 9 February: 'Another body – we think it's German, but no one is sure.' A further demonstration of range facilities took place on 16 April, but was interrupted when an unlucky shot struck the towing cable: 'Demo of new Dive Bomber Range. Main cable broke when hit.' The Canadians did not use only British and American tanks – the Ram Tank was designed and manufactured in Montreal and one of these [unit unknown] was firing at the range on 21 April to test modifications.

There was another constraint to the firing schedule – allied aircraft whose flight paths crossed Birling Gap. This caused a closure on 14 February prompting Manbert to note: 'Hope the army can come to an agreement with RAF – our range is as important as the flying of their bombers.' There was a further shut-down the following month when a Typhoon fighter was hit out at sea in front of the range. However, it was soon established that another aircraft was to blame for damage to the fighter and firing was allowed to continue.

In the confined space of the Belle Tout dugout, the car engine pulling the targets overheated. Mechanics had their work cut out to ensure it was kept running, and warmer weather made things intolerable. On 15 March it is noted: 'Men punched a hole in the rear of the Belle Tout engine room to keep everyone cool. Motorcycle dispatch riders carried details of the firing schedules between Birling Gap and the naval detachment at Newhaven. The journey would have taken no more than 20 minutes, yet: 'We've been having trouble with our dispatch rider service as the seaward warning is so important and required by Newhaven at least a week ahead of shoot. This place is so secret the dispatch riders can't find it.'

Captain Manbert and his men were keen observers of Channel shipping. The Diary entry for 17 March 1943 reads: 'Last night about 40 small ships sailed past our camp going east. I hope all the movements on the water fool Jerry as much as they do us.' It is possible that these vessels were part of the flotilla of assault landing craft mentioned on page 132. If so they may well have been heading for Eastbourne and/or Hastings Pier.

The range party was responsible for feeding the hundreds of artillerymen who came to fire. Two pre-war buildings at Birling Gap, the Children's Delight and the Golf House, served as kitchens; meals were eaten in Nissen huts nearby. On 17 February 1943, there were four extra mouths to feed when AA defences were stiffened along the coast: 'Four AA gunners from [British] LAA 19th Regiment and 463 Searchlight Battery were attached to us for quarters. They are posted here as part of the general scheme to strengthen our defences against Tip and Run Raids on the south coast towns. Planes approach at water level and skim over the cliff and hedge-hop their way to Eastbourne.'

The range party wasted no food. Anything not eaten became swill for their two pigs. Such bins were all around the town and in summer got rather smelly! The above picture is from the collection of the Imperial War Museum, number HU 36203.

From time to time the range party faced an unexpected crisis. Already on 26 February it is noted: 'Problems in the hutted camps because more personnel arrived than we had expected – but we sorted it out. We need two more Nissen huts.' A month later Manbert complains: 'Our arrangements for handling anything above 150 overnight are terrible with such small cooking space and mess hall room. This creates confusion, which makes it impossible to check damage and place responsibility.'

All soldiers are dismissive about army food, but on 8 April the fare was enough to tempt The Queens Own Cameron Highlanders of Canada [Anti-Tank Platoon, with 6-pounders] to eat first and shoot later. However, this was a bad move – at midday the range was closed for the afternoon. As a result, the Camerons were obliged to bivouac overnight in Horseshoe Plantation, the copse below Belle Tout. No doubt a lot of food had gone to waste, but a solution is noted on 19 April: 'Two pigs purchased by permission of District Agricultural Officer. They'll be fed on swill.'

The drains at Birling Gap had never been designed to cope with such large numbers and were a constant problem. On May 15, there were more difficulties when they got blocked up again at the Children's Delight and the Golf House. Already in mid-February an entry had recorded: 'With our small staff it's not easy to find spare hands for odd jobs, especially when some are on leave.' Visiting troops could be allocated tasks, but were not always co-operative: 'The Essex Scottish refused to clear out ditches but the matter was not reported until the men had left.' Another instance of poor discipline occurred when a soldier took advantage of a pause in firing to try to drive through the area after some lunchtime drinks: 'A drunken private of The Hastings and Prince Edward Regiment crashed a Jeep through our easterly roadblock at noon. Only the fact that we were closed for lunch prevented him from getting into serious difficulties.' The roadblock was at Shooters Bottom where a farm track still crosses the road.

It was possible for troops stationed at Birling Gap to get to the Winter Garden in Eastbourne, but entertainment was closer to hand on 23 April when a dance was organised at the Beachy Head Hotel. Forty-five WAAFs from Eastbourne and ten from Friston airfield were bussed in: 'A good time was had by all, but girls outnumbered the men.'

The Canadians at the artillery range would have been some of the first to witness the arrival of low-flying fighter-bombers. As mentioned on page 106, Eastbourne suffered a heavy raid on Sunday 7 March. Captain Manbert writes: '12 Fw-190s came in via the Belle Tout range and dropped three or four small bombs near the Beachy Head Hotel. We saw a couple of bombs leaving the racks. Two of the raiders were shot down over the sea by the RAF.' However, this is not borne out by *Luftwaffe Fighter-Bombers over Britain,* which notes a raid by 18 Fw-190s and no losses.[81] During a pause between work and raids, one man found peace in his vegetable garden: 'Gunner Bukovich is getting a small garden into shape, which will help out on the greens.'

The fighter-bombers were back on 3 April 1943 when the Park Gates Hotel was bombed, and a shelter in Spencer Road destroyed. The War Diary records: 'At 11.30, six Fw-190 came in in two close flights of three at 50 feet directly over Commandant's office [Birling Gap Hotel]. A minute or so later, the sounds of bombs indicated that the probable target was Eastbourne.' The last Tip and Run Raid took place on 6 June 1943: 'The Luftwaffe paid us a visit today. One Fw-190 brought down before they reached here and one of the seven or eight who passed over was smoking badly. Two minor casualties.' In course of this attack, cannon and machine-gun fire was directed at the Royal Observer Corps post at Beachy Head and LAA sites around the town. Over 100 holes were counted in the Royal Observer Corps lookout hut.[82] In an attempt to disguise targets such as Newhaven, decoy fires were sometimes lit. It must have been one of these which the range party saw on the night of 14 March: 'At 0030hrs the whole of Birling Gap and the surrounding countryside was lit up by a dozen large fires, which gave a very weird effect to the Downs.'

On 7 June 1943, Manbert may still have been feeling uncomfortable after an embarrassing encounter the previous day:

'I should have mentioned yesterday that Sir James Purves-Stewart, the owner of Belle Tout Lighthouse, came with Lt Col Stevenson of the Army Ordnance Corps to see what damage had been done to his place. I fear he was given a nasty shock, as the building is getting to the point where it will have to be completely rebuilt. He has asked to have a picture taken and Mr Arch [a local resident and artist] *was instructed by me to take one today. The Clerk of Works, Mr*

Moss and his assistant, Mr Hart, came down to see what damage had been done by the enemy raiders and also to check on our new kitchen stove.'

Belle Tout Lighthouse – a view of the ruin taken shortly after the war by John Donne for *Sussex County Magazine*. The lighthouse functioned from 1828-1902, but was sold to Sir James Purves-Stewart in 1923 and converted into a house. The damage was caused by stray shots aimed at wooden targets in the form of tanks which ran up a railway line immediately to the east of the building.

The photograph arrived the next day and was sent to Sir James with a bill for 12/6! Sir James must have made his displeasure felt – on 24 June there was a visit from officers of South East Command and the War Department Land Agents Office. They had come to see what was to be done about Sir James Purves-Stewart's lighthouse home. They decided that salvage was useless – the damage was considered total. It was planned to send a truck to pick up the odd thing which Sir James might value.*

---

* In *Beachy Head,* John Surtees writes that Sir James Purves-Stewart received £5,000 in compensation. The tower remained a ruin until rebuilding started in 1956. Sir James never returned to live at Belle Tout.

144

Captain Manbert went off for nine days' leave on 7 July, and two days later there was a break to the routine:

'We were visited by a Commando unit who arrived complete with balloons, a truckload of hydrogen, coils of rope etc. Apparently the idea is to practise cliff scaling by flying a balloon from the beach to a point over the top of the cliff and then clambering up the cliff face on a rope from the balloon, a horrifying plan to us run of the mill soldiers. There is a particularly high wind today which just seems to add zest to the proceedings – one unfortunate youth was hoisted about 30 feet into the air when a balloon broke away. Luckily he decided to drop off when he did, or he would still be flying, probably over London by now.

Again visited by the Commandos who arrived this morning [10 July] *with a bewildering variety of equipment – great hooks and what looked like grappling irons, a collapsible kayak, another larger folding boat and quite a lot of assorted explosives. They ran about all morning assembling and taking their equipment apart again and again while their officers issued incomprehensible (to us) orders. No balloons have broken away today, and nor have any of their boys fallen over the cliff though we cannot imagine why not as they take fearsome risks clambering about. They are all exceedingly tough and an efficient looking crowd.*

The Commandos visited us again [12 July] *plus air force, navy and marines, also a rather bewildered looking American captain who rushed about clasping a movie camera and taking shots from queer angles in the best Hollywood tradition. They lost no balloons today, but succeeded in puncturing one on a hook. I'm sure this training is beneficial but it's very rough on balloons.'*

July 13 was an important day for the range party as they got ready to demonstrate the blowing of gun pits. It was also proposed to fire 40mm AA guns at prepared barbed wire positions. Two

Brigade Royal Artillery officers and numerous staff officers were expected to attend. Manbert confesses: 'Such demonstrations throw everyone into a fever of anxiety lest something go wrong.' What a relief it must have been that there had been no hitches and that the top brass pronounced themselves pleased with the demonstration.

The War Diary for 1 June 1943 states: 'Brigadier Costin, CO Sussex Sub District, under whose command comes the 55th (British) Division, including the 165th Brigade, has taken over the area from Canadian troops.' Then, on 23 June, there is an entry stating that the range would be handed over to the School of Artillery. On 10 August, the War Diary of No 1 Canadian School of Artillery (Overseas) notes that they had taken control, operating the ranges from their HQ at Seaford College. During the autumn, refurbishment and reconstruction was carried out and firing continued until the end of 1944 at least. The Canadian School of Artillery was disbanded at Seaford on 21 September 1945, by which time most of its personnel would have been in the repatriation stream, homeward bound across the Atlantic. However, local authorities must have feared that the refurbished ranges might be there to stay for, on 26 September, a resolution is noted in the CBOE minutes stating that there would be a protest at any suggestion that the ranges on the Downs might be made permanent.

At the end of the war, German POWs dismantled the railway which had carried the targets. Eddie Williams, then a schoolboy living at Bullock Down Farm, remembers that the prisoners constructed a makeshift ladder from chestnut fencing and climbed down the cliff for a swim during their lunch break.

23

And we're self-propelled, too

In telling the story of the Canadian soldiers and how they and Eastbourne interacted during the war, it is important not to overlook the bigger picture. What had they done before they came? What happened to them after they left? To deal with these aspects we will look at one unit already mentioned above. *The History of The 23rd Canadian Field Regiment (SP) RCA* was written by Lieutenant L N Smith and published after the war. He served with the Regiment from its inception until VE Day and beyond – the summary which follows is drawn from his work.

The story really begins in April 1942, at Petawawa Camp in Ontario, when three field batteries came together to form a new regiment of The Royal Canadian Artillery, The 23rd Field Regiment, RCA. All three were raised in the Province of Ontario. The 31st Field Battery was from Toronto; then came the 36th Field Battery from Cobourg, and finally the 83rd Field Battery from Hamilton, Brantford and St Catherine's. In charge was Lieutenant Colonel J A Robertson, a veteran of the Great War, who had returned from England to take command. It was Robertson's task to mould these three entities into a regiment.

The spring and summer days at Petawawa were hot, uncomfortable and demanding – documentation, vaccinations, drill, first aid, lectures and all the other aspects of military life that have to be drummed in before a civilian starts to become a soldier. But what is an artillery regiment without its guns? It was not until eight towed 25-pounders were delivered that the men felt they were gunners. At the same time, the individual batteries were broken down into two four-gun troops and a headquarters troop. Competition was encouraged and the various troops vied with each other to attain perfection in gun drill and live firing. Towards July, rumours began to circulate – the Regiment was on the move. Initial stories that they would be going to the Pacific were proved wrong when it was announced that the destination was Sussex – not Sussex, England, but Camp Sussex in New Brunswick, near the Atlantic coast. The Regiment continued training in this location for the next eleven months.

Early in 1943, a fundamental change took place in the way the Regiment would operate. Instead of towing the guns, it would be equipped with self-propelled artillery pieces. These were 25-pounders mounted on the chassis of a Ram tank. The latter was designed and made in Canada, but never used as such in action. However, the Ram proved its worth when converted into a self-propelled gun. The biggest problem was one of drivers – and in February a large number of officers and men embarked on a course in tank driving. The conversion from 'towed' to 'self-propelled' also involved several changes of name. This finally ended up as The 23rd Field Regiment (SP) RCA. The two letters in brackets gave rise to some confusion, with mail arriving for The 23rd Special Police Regiment! The first of the new SP mounts was delivered early in April, just after the arrival of a new CO, Lieutenant Colonel K N Lander.

Lieutenant Smith's narrative explains that the New Brunswick Department of Highways was none too pleased when these new tracked monsters started chewing up its roads and knocking down bridges. The matter was further complicated because no one knew for sure how the wooden bridges would stand up to a Sexton, which weighed some 25 tons. The route of the SP mounts was always traced the following day by a road and fence repair party who were responsible for making good any damage.

On 20 July 1943, the Regiment moved to Halifax, Nova Scotia, where the Queen Elizabeth was waiting to transport them – and 16,000 others – across the Atlantic in a four-day unescorted dash. Every available corner of the great liner was crammed with troops. The men were served with two huge meals each day, spending 24 hours on deck and the next 24 in cabins.

RMS Queen Elizabeth packed with soldiers in her wartime trooping role. The great liner lay uncompleted in the Clyde when war broke out. On 3 March 1940, she raced unescorted across the Atlantic. After fitting out had been completed in New York and Singapore, she was involved in trooping duties from November 1942 until 1946.

On 27 July the 'Lizzie' slipped into Gourock harbour in Scotland. The time was 2030 hours – the Regiment was overseas. At the quayside, Scottish housewives served tea and buns to the men as they waited to board the trains that would carry them to Sunningdale in Surrey. From here trucks took them to a reception camp on Chobham Common pending their departure for Eastbourne. Their stay by the sea is described in Chapter 5 – Eastbourne was to be their home until 17 March 1944, when they moved to Pippingford Park near Nutley.

After the creature comforts of Eastbourne, Pippingford – a muddy couple of acres, filled with trees and Nissen huts – came as a shock. However, the Regiment was brought closer together – in Eastbourne, things had been organised on a battery basis. Now messes were set up for officers and sergeants, and there was a Regimental NAAFI and YMCA. Contact with the outside world was not easy – the nearest pub was four miles away at Nutley; East Grinstead was twelve miles distant.

In May 1944 the order was given for vehicles to be waterproofed; the scent of invasion and forthcoming combat was in the air. Towards the end of June, the Regiment went under canvas on a stretch of open ground between Wych Cross and Chelwood Gate. Although men could obtain 24-hour passes, travel was restricted to a 20-mile radius. However, by requesting travel passes to Purley and Polegate, some made it to London and Eastbourne for brief visits. At 2300 hours on 18 July 1944, a tracked convoy left for a holding camp on Wandsworth Common, the wheeled vehicles following four hours later. After embarkation, they spent several days at anchor in the Thames estuary, finally sailing for Normandy on the evening of 24 July. They landed from LCTs [Landing Craft Tank] on 26 July not far from Meauvaines some seven weeks after D-Day.

By 28 July, recce parties were moving towards Caen to relieve the British 7th Armoured Division, the Desert Rats. Facing them was the cream of the German army, thickened with SS and Panzer troops; it was in this sector that 23 Fd Regt discovered what it was like to be on the receiving end of artillery fire. The stage was set for a move by British, Canadian and Polish forces known as Operation Totalize. This was preceded by bombing and an artillery barrage – their guns were busier that night than ever before. In the morning, the men saw for the first time the consequences of modern warfare – smashed buildings and the sun-blackened bodies of German and Allied troops. And as the day wore on, the Regiment suffered its first casualty – ironically a victim of friendly fire from heavy bombers of the USAAF.

On 10 August, the column was shelled; the RHQ office truck was demolished and the first of the troops lost his life due to enemy action. The following day, the CO, Lt-Col Lander, received a back injury when he fell from his tank when the Brigade was under fire. This injury was so serious that he was transferred to England and thence to Canada. However, the Regiment gradually advanced and, after the fall of Falaise, was ready to start on the run across France. They passed through Bernay on the afternoon of 24 August to be greeted with flowers and fruit from the population; in return, cigarettes and chocolate were thrown into the crowds. The gunners caught sight of a mob marching collaborators up the main street, and women who had been friendly with Germans having their heads shaved. After further action on 2 September, the column was given a period of rest during which maintenance was carried out.

The Canadian 4th Armoured Division and 23 Fd Regt were on the road again on 6 September with Holland as the destination. They passed to the south of Dunkirk, where the Germans were holding out in some strength. By 8 September they had entered Belgium, but suffered further casualties. The ancient city of Bruges was spared the destruction of artillery fire, although several air-bursts were directed at bridges to encourage the departure of the defenders. A period of static warfare followed; the men even had time for 24-hour passes to Ghent. The advance continued, with the unit taking more casualties during the move towards Antwerp.

The above is not a lament for gunners of 23 Fd Regt, but for 55 members of A Company of the Black Watch at Ossendrecht in Holland on 26 Oct 1944. It could well be that the pipers at the gravesides were some of those who escorted the Mayor through Eastbourne on 22 November 1941. See page 73.

The column fought its way into Holland and, on 7 November, there began a dull period when they 'held the line' along the River Maas awaiting a spring offensive. December 25 was spent on the outskirts of Breda, and most of the men managed to enjoy a Christmas dinner in schools and other buildings.

By 25 January, and in sub-zero temperatures, 23 Fd Regt had reached a point to the north-east of Tilburg, and were in action firing an intricate barrage, first of smoke shells and then HE, in support of infantry. On 22 February, the column moved towards the Rhine. There were more casualties on the night of 1-2

March as the Allied force pushed through a gap. The tanks of the Forward Observation Officers came under heavy fire – one was reported missing; another FOO was temporarily blinded and the tank of a third FOO set ablaze.

The vehicles of 23 Fd Regt crossed the Rhine into Germany on the morning of Easter Sunday 1945. On 10 April the column beat off a counter-attack by German paratroopers, but incurred further losses. A period of movement across difficult terrain followed until the town of Bad Zwischenahn was taken on 1 May.

Reports of the death of Hitler filtered through, together with confirmation of the end of Mussolini; on 3 May, the Canadian 4th Armoured Division set out in hot pursuit of the enemy. The following evening, news was received that all enemy forces in north-western Germany, Denmark and Holland had surrendered to 21 Army Group. Then on 5 May came the welcome words – 'Cease Fire'. The Regiment had fired its last round and reached the end of a long trail. But 25 of its officers and men had lost their lives along the way.[83]

24
Thanks for the memory

All the soldiers who passed through Eastbourne were volunteers. But why did they do it? In the early days, few would have felt that Canada was directly threatened. The horrors of the First World War were well documented and would have been vividly described by fathers and uncles. Some men would have volunteered because of family ties with Britain; others for idealistic reasons. There would have been those who joined because their friends had done so. No doubt some wanted to test themselves. Others may have sought escape from a boring job or unemployment. Many could have been seeking adventure overseas. In any event, the Canadian Army played a key role in the Second World War – and we were extremely fortunate to have had them at our side.

The last of the Canadians would have left Eastbourne in 1944. The friendly 'occupation' had lasted some three years. Any of those former soldiers must now be over 80 years of age – the minimum age for service overseas was nineteen. When this project was started in the 1980s, a letter to *Legion*, the Canadian ex-servicemen's magazine, produced a good number of replies. From time to time, the phone would ring announcing a veteran on a trip to Europe and suggesting a drink at the Ship or the Pilot.

In 2004, an appeal for information in an Ontario newspaper, and another in *Legion,* produced only a handful of letters – and two of those were from widowed war brides. The descendants of Eastbourne's 151 war brides have roots in what was called 'a south coast town of no military significance'. Now, apart from the eroding names etched in the garden wall of the Moorings, little visible evidence remains of the wartime Canadian presence.

Yet older residents of Meads will swear that on a quiet evening they can still hear the clatter of caterpillar tracks – and the sound of Bombardier Stan Watkins playing the piano in the Saloon Bar of the Pilot.

Abbreviations

AA	Anti-aircraft
AHQ	Army Headquarters
ALC	Assault Landing Craft
BHQ	Battalion Headquarters
CBOE	County Borough of Eastbourne
CMHQ	Canadian Military Headquarters
CO	Commanding Officer
CWAC	Canadian Women's Army Corps
Fd Regt	Field Regiment
FOO	Forward Observation Officer
Fw	Focke-Wulf
HPER	Hastings and Prince Edward Regiment
IWM	Imperial War Museum
JG	Jagdgeschwader (Fighter Group)
Ju	Junkers
LAA	Light Anti-Aircraft
LMG	Light Machine-gun
Me	Messerschmitt
NAAFI	Navy Army and Air Force Institutes
NFS	National Fire Service
OP	Observation Post
PPCLI	Princess Patricia's Canadian Light Infantry
QOR	Queen's Own Rifles of Canada
RCA	Royal Canadian Artillery
RCAF	Royal Canadian Air Force
RCAMC	Royal Canadian Army Medical Corps
RCCS	Royal Canadian Corps of Signals
RCE	Royal Canadian Engineers
RCEME	Royal Canadian Elect. & Mech. Engineers
RCOC	Royal Canadian Ordnance Corps
RCR	Royal Canadian Regiment
RHQ	Regimental Headquarters
SP	Self-Propelled
USAAF	United States Army Air Force
WAAF	Women's Auxiliary Air Force
WRNS	Women's Royal Naval Service ('Wrens')
YMCA	Young Men's Christian Association
YWCA	Young Women's Christian Association

Acknowledgements

That something which started as a research project in the 1980s should have become a book is due to the help of many people. The names of some correspondents are credited within the body of the book, but it is impossible to mention all of those who have been so generous. Sadly, many of the original veterans who wrote with their memories will not see the publication of this book.

The assistance of the webmasters and contributors to two websites ('Canuck' www.canadiansoldiers.com and 'MLU' www.mapleleafup.org) cannot be overstated. It was through the latter that I got in touch with Mark W Tonner, CD, of London, Ontario, who is retired from The Royal Canadian Regiment. His encyclopaedic knowledge and vast personal archive of material about all aspects of the Canadian and British Armies have been of immense assistance.

For information on The Black Watch of Canada, I must thank Laird Niven of Dartmouth, Nova Scotia. Clifford Weirmeir, whose speciality is The Irish Regiment of Canada, has been generous with information from his study of accidents incurred by Canadian servicemen. Queries about LAA guns and units were promptly answered by Derek Barton, whose Royal Artillery website (www.ra39-45.pwp.blueyonder.co.uk) is a fine resource. Gratitude is due to David Fletcher, Historian of the Tank Museum (www.tankmuseum.co.uk). Emily Bird of Brookwood Cemetery kindly helped me to trace the Dempsey family, and thus establish the identity and solve the mystery of 'Gunner Lawrence'. The website (www.normandie44lamemoire.com) is devoted to the Canadian landings at Juno Beach; Philippe Corvé provided information and photographs of the memorials at Bernières-sur-Mer. Mike George obliged by taking photographs while I was abroad, and interviewing Babs Clements about her wartime memories. Nicholas Stevenson helped with photography when my scanner broke down. Various military museums have furnished information and helpful leads. In particular I am grateful to Joe

Costello, webmaster of the Royal Canadian Corps of Signals site (www.rcsigs.ca).

Finally, the members of Eastbourne Local History Society's Publications Sub-Committee have been kind enough to read through my manuscript and offer suggestions and corrections. I am especially grateful to Peter Longstaff-Tyrrell, who shares my interest in the Canadian presence in our area during the Second World War.

Appendix A

Location Statement Number 6 – Dated 11 August 1942

Location Statements give the positions of all units – Canadian and British. They were regularly amended and filed with Divisional or Brigade papers; civilian authorities also received copies and so they can sometimes be found at County Record Offices. The one below was issued by the 2nd Canadian Infantry Brigade upon its arrival in our area. This was prior to Dieppe and immediately before the night air raid on Upperton, where Canadian forces had just moved into their new quarters. The map references relate to wartime OS sheets, but for Eastbourne a correction can be obtained by adding 566812. However, this is not accurate further afield. Where no telephone number is given, it must be assumed that field telephones were used. The old GPO telephone numbers are sometimes 'transparent' – despite new exchanges and STD, vestiges may still exist. For example, the Cooden Beach Hotel is now 01424 842281. Unfortunately, overtyping and faded ink have left some characters in the Location Statement illegible.

Unit	Location	MR	Tel
HQ 2 Cdn Inf Bde	West Lords House, Willingdon	026203	Hampden Park 102
Defence Platoon, 2 Cnd Infantry Brigade	West Lords House, Willingdon	026203	ditto
K Section Signals	West Lords House, Willingdon	026203	ditto
2 Light Aid Detachment	Old Bus Terminal, Eastbourne	046183 (?)	

Appendix A

Unit	Location	MR	Tel
PPCLI, Battalion HQ	Malaya House, Willingdon	028204	Hampden Park 96
HQ Company	Caragana, Grand [sic] Rd Willingdon (in fact 'Brand')		
A Company	Hadleigh, Kings Dve, Willingdon	030205	Hampden Park 71
B Company	Little Dene, Kings Dve, Willingdon		Hampden Park 80
C Company	Big House, Willingdon		Hampden Park 136
D Company	Changla, Park Avenue, Willingdon	030202	Hampden Park 60
Seaforth of Canada, BHQ	Hankham House	046233	Westham 358 (?)
HQ Company		073233 (?)	
A Company		052233 (?)	
B Company		063239	
C Company		083237	
D Company		067209	
Edmonton Regiment, Battalion HQ	Prideaux Place, Prideaux Road, Eastbourne	039190	Eastbourne 3740/1
HQ Company	30 Carew Road, Eastbourne	036187	ditto
A Company	Manaos, Kings Drive, Eastbourne	039193	ditto
B Company	8 Carew Road, Eastbourne	037187	ditto
C Company	Merrivale, Ashburnham Road, Eastbourne	039189	ditto
D Company	31 Lewes Road, Eastbourne	043189	ditto

158

Appendix A

Unit	Location	MR	Tel
5 Cnd Fd Regt RCA, RHQ	Hurst Green	169457 (?)	Hurst Green 30
1 Canadian Anti-Tank Regiment	Cooden Beach Hotel	145251	Cooden 281
3 Canadian Field Company, RCE	St Martins Abbey	185343	Battle 406
9 Canadian Field Ambulance MDS	Crossways House	987286	Hellingly 327
A Company, 9 Cdn Field Ambulance ADS	Roborough School	045183	Eastbourne 209
2 Canadian LAA Regiment	Trevin Towers [Gaudick Road] Eastbourne	035170	Eastbourne 4660/1
A Company, Saskatoon Light Infantry (MG)	St Michael's Lodge, Uckfield	911393	Uckfield 376
HQ 1 Canadian Division	Heathfield Park	036397	Heathfield 282
HQ 1 Canadian Infantry Brigade	Horam Grange	014359	Horam Road 282
HQ 3 Canadian Infantry Brigade	Delves, Ringmer	883316	Ringmer 499
2 Cdn Field Hygiene Section	Quorn Lodge, Cowbeech	052322	Herstmonceux 1174
1 Canadian Mobile Bath	ditto	ditto	ditto
1 Canadian Provost Company	Nightengale [sic] Cottage	013254	Hailsham 39/375
1 Canadian Field Security	25 Ersham Road, Hailsham	025282	Hailsham 138
3 Canadian Postal Unit	Legion Hall, Cross in Hand	001406	Hailsham 138
1 Cdn Div Ordnance Workshop, 2 Group & HQ	Melford House, Crowborough	949498	Crowborough 638

Appendix A

Unit	Location	MR	Tel
1 Canadian Division Ordnance Dump	Poultry Co-op Packers Plant, Heathfield	025405	Heathfield 19
1 Canadian Ordnance Field Park	Coopers Green	915420	Buxted 234
2 Canadian Mobile Laundry & Forward Decontamination Unit	Frant	028560 (?)	Frant 12
3 Canadian Salvage Unit	Buxted	933422	Buxted 217
1 Cdn Division Section Canadian Corps Recreation Camp	Mountfield Lodge, Mountfield Road, Lewes	850290	Lewes 436
ALC School		945168	Seaford 3184
1 Cdn Army (2-pounder) Anti-tank School	Birling Gap		Eastdean 3307
1 Canadian Dental Company	Stonebridge House	957390	Framfield 234
Claims Office	Roselea, Summerfield Avenue, Hailsham	850290	
14 Canadian Tank Battalion	The Towers, Seaford	927183	Seaford 3345
3 Battery, 56 (?) Heavy Regiment, RA	Hardwycke, Hailsham	024281	Hailsham 368
19 Super Heavy Battery, RA	Hailsham	024283	Hailsham 56
552 C Regiment, RA	Broadoak Manor	161271	Cooden 493
221 Coastal Battery,	Cooden	151253	Cooden 372
237 Coastal Battery	Pevensey Bay	091225	Pevensey 291
301 Coastal Battery	Bexhill	103258	Bexhill 494
342 Coastal Battery	Eastbourne	048169	Eastbourne 1275

Appendix A

Unit	Location	MR	Tel
360 Coastal Battery	Hastings	263279	Hastings 2365
375 Coastal Battery	Normans Bay	124245	Pevensey Bay 233
10 Defence Troop, RA	125 Royal Parade, Eastbourne	059189	Eastbourne 99
11 Defence Troop, RA	The Brink, Pevensey Bay	093225	Pevensey Bay 340
11 Armoured Division School	Southdown Hotel, Eastbourne		Eastbourne 1480/1608
D Troop 338 Searchlight Battery	Hurstmonceux	074301	Hurstmonceux 197
C Troop 331 (?) Searchlight Battery	The Grange, St Helens	284306	Hastings 3722
410 Light Anti-Aircraft Battery, RA	Friston	973168	Eastdean 267
5 (?) Light Anti-Aircraft Battery, RA	Friston	973158	Eastdean 267
30 Battalion Queen's (?)	Crossways	494212	Rustington 8678
7 Company	Collington Manor	162263	Bexhill 750
Unit Posts			
Beachy Head		023144	Eastbourne 1902
Wartling		092269	Hurstmonceux 217
Pevensey		083263 (?)	Hurstmonceux 217
Bexhill		062054	Cooden 279
Fairlight		195297 (?)	Pett 2174
		286302	Pett 3106

161

Appendix A

Unit	Location	MR	Tel
C Company	Old School House, Southern High Street, Lewes		
Friston Air Port [sic]	Crowlink	980165	East Dean 337
Naval Cadets Training School	St Bedes School, Eastbourne	035195	Eastbourne 1550
RAF Beachy Head		023144	Eastbourne 1902
RAF Pevensey		077257	Westham 353
RAF Friston (Regiment)		973168	East Dean 267
RAF 1 EANS	Sandhurst Hotel, Grand Parade, Eastbourne	048172	Eastbourne 3390
RAF Training Establishment	Marina Hotel, Hastings	236274	Hastings 4000
Home Guard			
20 (Hailsham) Battalion HQ	Ravenscourt, 46 Summerheath Road, Hailsham		Hailsham 213/4 Nights 311
21 (Eastbourne) Battalion HQ	Rosebank, Dittons Road, Eastbourne		Eastbourne 468
22 (Battle) Battalion HQ	Brickwall, Sedlescombe, Nr Battle		Sedlescombe 26
23 (Hastings) Battalion HQ	Oakhurst, 401 The Ridge, Hastings		Baldslow 343
ARP Controls			
Hailsham			Hailsham 206
Eastbourne			Eastbourne 4141
Bexhill			Bexhill 2617
Hastings			Hastings 5000

Appendix A

Unit	Location	MR	Tel
Police			
Eastbourne			Eastbourne 4141
Hailsham			Hailsham 31
Bexhill			Bexhill 946
Hastings			Hastings 5000
AQC, 51 High Street, Hailsham			Hailsham 251
Royal Observer Corps			
Observation Post	Hilders, Chiddingley	014260	Chiddingley 2
Coast Guard Stations			
Burling [sic] Gap		989147	East Dean 328
Beachy Head (Naval Signals)		024415 (?)	Eastbourne 328
Holywell Bay		037159	Eastbourne 5069
Langley [sic] Point		077196	Eastbourne 931
Pevensey Bay		092226	Pevensey 278
Cooden		143251	Cooden 554
Bexhill		176256	Bexhill 797
St Leonards			Bexhill 1258
Hastings			Hastings 1125
Naval Officer i/c Newhaven			Newhaven 72
Officer i/c Coast Guard, Newhaven			Newhaven 72
139 Infantry Brigade (Br)	Orchard House	351455	Wittersham 2

Signed C. Vokes (Brigadier), Commander 2 Canadian Infantry Brigade

Appendix B
Known LAA Sites in and around Eastbourne
(Incomplete List)
August 1942, Sites for Static Use
54th Battery and 2nd (Yorkton) Battery,
2 Canadian LAA Regiment RCA

MR	Approximate Position	MR	Approximate Position
598986	Golf Links	595971	Well Combe
595966	Above Whitbread Hollow,	612980	Western Lawns
633005	Near Leisure Pool	598970	Above Foot Beachy Head

During Operation Order 'Duckshooting' from 23 October 1942
(See Page 117)
British 27 AA Brigade RA, Sites for Static Use
(40mm Bofors unless indicated otherwise)

MR	Approximate Position	MR	Approximate Position
591986	Hill above Fairway Close	635007	Prince William Parade
592009	Ocklynge School	622997	By Redoubt Tea Rooms
600005	Claxton Close	623996	By Redoubt Tea Rooms
611006	Tutts Barn Lane	619988	Pier
620014	Caffyns Hammond Drive	608784	Out of local area
623016	Alder Close	609979	Corner of St Johns Rd and South Cliff
630017	Near The Circus	605975	Seafront lawns by Kepplestone
635013	Mountbatten Drive	598971	Above Upper Dukes Drive
545983	(For Friston Airfield) Near South Hill	543967	(For Friston Airfield) South of Crowlink
541978	(For Friston Airfield) Near Gayles,	524975	(For Friston Airfield) Near Cliff End
533974	(For Friston Airfield) Near Gayles	532979	(For Friston Airfield) (Quad Lewis Gun) Near Gayles
539986	(For Friston Airfield) North of A 259	533985	(For Friston Airfield) (Quad Lewis Gun) Near Exceat New Barn
638076	(For Radar Station) Manxey Level	654068	(For Radar Station) Near Chilley
648062	(For Radar Station) Near Chilley	648078	(For Radar Station) (Quad Lewis Gun) Near Chilley

During Operation Order 'Duckshooting' from 23 October 1942
(See Page 117)
2 Canadian LAA Regiment RCA,
Sites for Mobile Use – some may have become Static

MR	Approximate Position	MR	Approximate Position
610979	Promenade nr Grand	600988	Golf Links
603973	Helen Gardens	593974	Above Cranbourne Ave
587974	Black Robin Farm	589984	Above Foredown Close
604976	Chesterfield Road	592991	Upland Road
599982	St Rita's Paradise Dve	639008	Prince William Parade
601980	Sunnymead, Gaudick Rd	630005	Princes Park
595975	Aldro, Darley Rd	620999	Seaside Recreation Gnd
597981	Behind Moira House	619009	Churchdale Place
593967	Road Nr Bullock Down	632036	Hide Hollow Farm
596958	Above Cow Gap	633045	Westham, Mt Pleasant
581954	Above BH Lighthouse	641039	Mill Ditch
576962	East of Bulling Dean	643047	Nr Pevensey Castle
571956	Hodcombe Farm	647027	Crumbles
559964	Nr Birling Gap	652036	Pev Bay, Timberlaine Rd
559964	Nr Birling Farm	656041	Pev Bay, Castle Dve
547968	Nr Crowlink	661043	Pevensey Bay
486986	Seaford	677057	Rockhouse Bank
494980	Seaford Head	680055	Rockhouse Bank
501977	Seaford, South Hill	695061	Normans Bay
511976	Cuckmere Estuary	701060	Cooden
467005	Seaford	685076	Hooe, Old Road Farm
474996	Seaford	689074	Hooe, Old Road Farm
479991	Seaford	691079	Hooe
482990	Seaford	697080	Bexhill, Barnhorn Manor

June 1943
53rd Battery, 11 Canadian LAA Regiment RCA, Sites for Static Use

MR	Approximate Position	MR	Approximate Position
617018	Lottbridge Drove	643011	Langney Point
606010	Near DGH	622026	West Langney Level
583004	Polegate Playing Field	590962	Downs, Heathy Brow
584997	Downs, Middle Brow	593980	Nr Paradise Reservoir
582955	Downs, The Peak	596962	Downs, Nr Cow Gap
589971	Downs, Nr Black Robin	599970	Downs above St Bedes

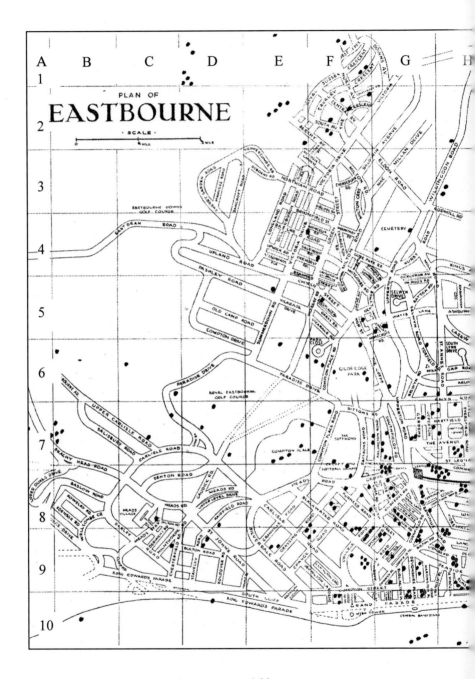

PLAN OF
EASTBOURNE
· SCALE ·

Key to plan of Eastbourne

The plan on pages 166 – 167 is from *Eastbourne 1939 to 1945*, published by Strange the Printer after the war. The black dots show where bombs fell, and it is easy to see why Eastbourne became known as 'The most raided town in the South East'.

The cluster of bombs in J-9 fell around Bourne Street, which was called 'Hell Fire Corner'. It was here that the army created the Eastbourne Street Fighting School. Although paddle steamers used to sail to France from the Victorian pier (H-10), it has never been a commercial jetty. It was a frequent target, but survived the war. The generating station and old gasometers were singled out by Fw-190 fighter-bombers in Roselands (M-7 & N-7).

Meads (A-7/10 to D-7/10) was developed by the Duke of Devonshire in the 19th century and is characterised by large detached houses, some of which were private schools. Both categories were taken over by the army and used by 2 Fd Regt, 23 Fd Regt, 2 LAA and the Black Watch. Two popular pubs with Canadians – the Ship and the Pilot – still thrive in Meads Street (C-9). The RCCS radio vans were on high ground in B-6 and A-7, and later at Chaseley in D-9. The Devonshire Baths (F-10) are gone. Belle Tout lighthouse and Beachy Head are off the map to the west. Upperton (G-4/7 to J-4/7) is a mixture of large Victorian properties and inter-war housing – it was home to the Calgaries, the Edmontons, the HPER, the Irish Regiment, the Perths and the Toronto Scottish. Many of these men drank at the Tally-Ho in F-4.

Hampden Park and Willingdon (above H-1 to N-1) were taken by the Black Watch, PPCLI, QOR and the Seaforths. Westlords (above H-1) was a Brigade HQ and is now flats; Malaya House in Park Lane (J-1) was BHQ of several regiments. Ratton Manor (above F-1 to G-1) is gone and its grounds have been developed. The Chaudières and Maisonneuves were mainly at Pevensey, Westham and Stone Cross, which lie off the map to the east.

Picture credits

Every effort has been made to clear copyright but the source of some pictures is obscure; some are from organisations which no longer exist. The publication of any picture for which copyright clearance has not been granted is unintentional. It is hoped that appearance in this book will be seen as a tribute to the men of the Canadian Army who served in Eastbourne during the Second World War. Pictures which are not credited are from the author's collection.

Front Cover – Recruiting Poster *(Courtesy Library and Archives Canada/Accession no. 1983-30-236)*, Rear Cover – Westminster Regiment *(DND-1967-52, Beachy Head)* & Recruiting Poster *(Courtesy of the Canadian Department of National Defence and Canadian War Museum ©CWM)*, Pier *(Hurst)*, page 1 – Powell House *(Eastbourne College)*, page 3 – Poster *(Courtesy Library and Archives of Canada)*, page 9 – London I cannot leave you *(Noel Gay)*, page 11 – Ratton Manor *(Around Eastbourne by Patricia Berry & Kevin Gordon - Sutton Publishing 1996, via Longstaff-Tyrrell)*, page 12 – Headline *(Eastbourne Chronicle)*, page 13 – Black Watch Battle Drill RHC near Eastbourne 7.3.42 Royal, *(Reproduced with the permission of the Minister of Public Works and Government Services Canada, 2006)*, page 15 – Home Guard *(Eastbourne Public Library, Hudson)*, page 19 – Sexton *(www.tanxheaven.com – Schoot)*, page 21 – Veterans *(Herb Danter)*, page 23 – Sherman *(Eastbourne 1939 – 1945, Strange the Printer)*, page 24 – Officers at Bydown *(Murphy)*, page 25 – Buick *(Mackay)*, page 26 – Advertisement *(Sara Lee)*, page 28 – Murphy Bros & Couple *(Murphy)*, page 30 – Shoulder to Shoulder Nr 19880069-860 *(Courtesy of the Canadian War Museum ©CWM)*, page 31 – Cartoon *(Courtesy of the Canadian Forces, Bing Coughlin)*, page 33 – Thayendanegea *(Canadian Heritage Gallery)*, page 34 – Wedding *(Fennell)*, page 35 – RMS Mauritania *(www.rmstitanic.dk, Madsen)*, page 38 – Winter Garden *(Eastbourne Gazette)*, page 40 – Cartoon *(Courtesy of the Canadian Forces, Bing Coughlin)*, page 44 – Poster by Mount *(IWM)*, page 47 – Memorial *(www.normandie44lamemoire.com, Philippe Corvé)*, page 51 – L Dempsey *(Dempsey)*, page 53 – Tally Ho *(Illustrated – IPC Media)*, page 56 – Pilot in WW2 and L Holleran *(Holleran)*, page 57 – Advertisement *(Eastbourne 1939 – 1945, Strange the Printer)*, page 59 – Stan Scislowski *(Scislowski)*, page 62 – Concert Party *(Tin Hats, Finale of their show in London on 9 October, 1941, DHist, DND, 5043, Department of National Defence. Reproduced with the permission of the Minister of Public Works and Government Services Canada, 2006.)*, page 63 – Headline *(Eastbourne Chronicle)*, page 66 – Canteen at Eastbourne – *(DHist, DVD, 3-15 A. Louis Jarché, Department of National Defence. This image reproduced with permission the Minister of Public Works and Govt Svcs, Ottawa, Canada, 2006)*,

Bibliography

The first point of reference for anyone interested in the history of the Canadian forces in Britain during the Second World War must be *The Half-Million – The Canadians in Britain, 1939-1946* by C P Stacey and Barbara M Wilson (University of Toronto Press). As a Major, C P Stacey gained first hand knowledge through his experience as Historical Officer at the Canadian Military HQ in London during the war. Barbara Wilson is an archivist at the Public Archives of Canada.

No attempt has been made to include a bibliography of Canadian unit histories, but a comprehensive list can be found at www.canadiansoldiers.com. This is under constant review, with new titles being added all the time.

Eastbourne Chronicle
Eastbourne Gazette
Eastbourne Herald
Kelly's Directories of Eastbourne
Pike's Blue Book, Eastbourne, Hailsham and District
Quarterly Journals of Eastbourne Local History Society
(*Eastbourne Local Historian*) and Eastbourne Society (formerly Eastbourne Civic Society)

Allom V M (1966) *Ex Oriente Salus – A Centenary History of Eastbourne College* (Eastbourne: Eastbourne College)
Barnard, Lt Col W T (ED CD) *The Queen's Own Rifles of Canada: 1860-1960 – One Hundred Years of Canada* (Don Mills, Ontario: Ontario Publishing Company)
Burgess P & Saunders A (1995) *Bombers over Sussex* (Midhurst: Middleton Press)
Calder R (2004) *A Richer Dust – Family, Memory and the Second World War* (Canada: Viking)
Clegg H (1942) *A Canuck in England* (London: Harrap & Co)
Copp T (1992) *The Brigade – The Fifth Canadian Infantry Brigade, 1939-1945 (*Stony Creek Ontario: Fortress Publications)

Costello J (1985) *Love Sex and War – Changing Values 1939-45* (London: Collins)

Dobinson C (2001) *AA Command* (London: Methuen)

Donne J (1947) *Sussex County Magazine*

Elliston R A (1999) *Eastbourne's Great War* (Seaford: SB Publications)

Forty G (1998) *British Army Handbook 1939-1945* (Phoenix Mill: Sutton Publishing)

Gates R & Weicker, Col C J *The Original Canadian Spies of the Airwaves* (Canada: Communications and Electronics, Department of National Defence)

Goss C (2003) *Luftwaffe Fighter-Bombers over Britain – The Tip and Run Campaign, 1942-43* (Manchester: Crécy)

Grant, Maj R S (MD, CD) & Weir, Cpt N A (CD) (1986) *Second World War Canadian Army Signals Intelligence Experiences* (Ottawa: Canadian Forces Communications and Electronics Newsletter 446)

Hardy N W (1945) *Eastbourne 1939-1945* (Eastbourne: Strange the Printer)

Henry H G Jr & Pallud J-P (1993) *Dieppe through the Lens* (London: Battle of Britain Prints International)

Hibbert J (1980) *The War Brides* (Winnipeg: Signet)

Hodges P R (1994) *Temples of Dreams* (Seaford: SB Publications)

Huggett C (1995) *Drusillas Railway – 60 Years of Narrow Gauge* (Alfriston: Drusillas Zoo Park)

Humphrey G (1989) *Wartime Eastbourne* (Eastbourne: Beckett Features)

Kerry, Col A J & McDill, Maj W A (1966) *The History of the Corps of Royal Canadian Engineers – Vol 2.* (Canada: Military Engineering Institute of Canada)

Longstaff-Tyrrell P (1997) *Operation Cuckmere Haven* (Polegate: Gote House)

Longstaff-Tyrrell P with Berry P (2002) *The Maple Leaf Army in Britain* (Polegate: Gote House)

Milton R & Callaghan R (2005) *The Redoubt Fortress and Martello Towers of Eastbourne* (Eastbourne: Eastbourne Local History Society)

O'Hara P (1985) *From Romance to Reality* (Cobalt, Ontario: Highway Book Shop)

Ramsey W (1987) *The Blitz – Then and Now* (London: Battle of Britain Prints International)

Ramsey W (1995) *D-Day – Then and Now* (London: Battle of Britain Prints International)

Reynolds D (1995) *Rich Relations – The American Occupation of Britain, 1942-1945* (New York: Random House)

Scislowski S (1997) *Not all of Us Were Brave* (Canada: Dundurn Press)

Smith, Lt L N (1945) *History of The 23rd Field Regiment (SP) RCA – World War II* (Holland: 23rd Field Regiment)

Stacey C P (1955) *Six Years of War, The Official History of the Canadian Army in the Second World War* (Ottawa: Minister of National Defence)

Stacey C P & Wilson B M (1987) *The Half-Million – The Canadians in Britain, 1939 – 1946* (Toronto: University of Toronto Press)

Stevens G R et al (1945) *Princess Patricia's Canadian Light Infantry, 1919-1957* (Canada: Privately published by the Regiment)

Stevens W Ray (1993) *The Canadian Entertainers of World War 2* (Oakville: Mosaic Press 1993)

Surtees J (1997) *Beachy Head* (Seaford: SB Publications)

Vine W J (1978) *Old Willingdon* (Willingdon: Published by the author)

Endnotes

All quoted War Diaries are at The National Archives (formerly Public Record Office) at Kew under reference WO 179. CMHQ and AHQ reports are available at www.forces.gc.ca/hr/

After you've gone

[1] Allom V M (1966) *Ex Oriente Salus – A Centenary History of Eastbourne College*. Eastbourne: Eastbourne College
[2] Cant J (undated) *Staying at the Cavendish*. Unpublished recollections; Ockenden M (2004) *Where were Eastbourne's Ack Ack Guns?* Eastbourne Local Historian, Number 131; The National Archives AIR 28/711
[3] *History of the Devonshire Regiment* (Further details unknown)

We're on our way

[4] Stacey C P & Wilson B M (1987) *The Half-Million – The Canadians in Britain, 1939-1946*. Preface & Ch 1, Toronto: University of Toronto Press
[5] CMHQ Report 041
[6] ibid
[7] Elliston R A (1999) *Eastbourne's Great War*. Ch 14, Seaford: SB Publications

This desirable residence

[8] CMHQ Report 123

Collateral damage

[9] *Ratton and the Freeman-Thomases*. Eastbourne Local History Society Newsletter, Number 23
[10] AHQ Report 066

Caterpillar Tracks

[11] Smith, Lt L N (1945) *The History of the 23rd Field Regiment (SP) RCA – World War II*. Holland: 23rd Field Regiment
[12] ibid
[13] ibid

Something about a soldier

[14] Stacey C P (1955) *The Official History of the Canadian Army in the Second World War, Vol 1.* Ch 11, Ottawa: Minister of National Defence
[15] Stacey & Wilson, op cit, Ch 5
[16] ibid
[17] Hibbert J (1980) *The War Brides.* p 32 Winnipeg: Signet
[18] O'Hara P (1985) *From Romance to Reality.* p 297 Cobalt, Ontario: Highway Book Shop
[19] ibid

Just one of those things

[20] Stacey & Wilson, op cit, Ch 5
[21] Stacey & Wilson, op cit, Ch 4
[22] Stacey & Wilson, op cit, Ch 5

Hands across the ocean

[23] Author's Interview (13 December 2003)
[24] www.normandie44lamemoire.com
[25] Stacey & Wilson, op cit, Ch 2

Finding Gunner Lawrence

[26] National Archives of Canada, Court of Inquiry (21 April 1943) by order of Lt.Col. H.M. Hague, E.D., Comd, 2 Cdn Fd Regt, RCA, for the purpose of inquiring into and reporting upon the circumstances surrounding the fatal injuries received by G.49834 Gnr Dempsey, L.M. on or about 7 Apr 43.

Another day another dollar

[27] Stacey & Wilson, op cit, Ch 2
[28] Stacey & Wilson, op cit, Ch 6
[29] Hodges P R (1994) *Temples of Dreams.* p 63-64, Seaford: SB Publications

Marching on its stomach

[30] For details of Stan Scislowski's experiences in the Italian campaign with the Perth Regiment see *Not all of us were Brave* (1997) Canada: Dundurn Press

Forget all your troubles – and just get happy

[31] Stacey & Wilson, op cit, Ch 4
[32] ibid
[33] Clegg H (1942) *A Canuck in England*, London: Harrap & Co
[34] Stacey & Wilson, op cit, Ch 4
[35] Kefford W H (1990) 'The Tech – 1942-1957 and beyond': Personal Account
[36] Appendix to War Diary (23 July 1941) Le Régiment de Maisonneuve

Street fighting

[37] Saunders A (1982) *The Killing of Guardsman Fox*, After the Battle, Number 37

Read all about it

[38] Stacey & Wilson, op cit, Ch 6
[39] ibid
[40] ibid
[41] Official History of the Canadian Medical Services 1939-1945, Vol 2, Clinical Subjects

Frenchies

[42] Copp T (1992) *The Brigade – The Fifth Canadian Infantry Brigade, 1939-1945*. Ch 1, Stony Creek Ontario: Fortress Publications
[43] ibid
[44] ibid
[45] ibid
[46] Bernier S (1997) 'French Canadians in the Canadian Armed Forces in 1944'. *The Defence Associations National Network,* Vol 4, No 1
[47] ibid

In the field

[48] Copp T, op cit
[49] CMHQ Report 073
[50] Barnard Lt Col W T (ED CD), *The Queen's Own Rifles of Canada: 1860-1960, One Hundred years of Canada.* Don Mills, Ontario: Ontario Publishing Company (Grateful thanks to CWO Budden CD, Regimental Sgt Major of the QOR, for assistance with this source)
[51] Cant J, op cit
[52] CMHQ Report 123

Don't you know there's a war on?

[53] Stacey & Wilson, op cit, Ch 2
[54] HO 192/978 (The National Archives)
[55] Stevens G R et al, (1945) *Princess Patricia's Canadian Light Infantry, 1919-1957.* Canada: Privately published by the Regiment
[56] Goss C (2003) *Luftwaffe Fighter-Bombers over Britain – The Tip and Run Campaign, 1942-43.* Appendix 8, Manchester: Crécy
[57] Hardy N W (1945) *Eastbourne 1939-1945.* Eastbourne: Strange the Printer
[58] German Home Service, (8 March 1943) *BBC Written Archives, Caversham*
[59] Goss C, op cit, Appendix 8

Coming in for flak

[60] www.ra39-45.pwp.blueyonder.co.uk
[61] Goss C, op cit, Ch 5
[62] Cant J, op cit, Personal information
[63] Goss C, op cit, Ch 5
[64] Burgess P & Saunders A (1995) *Bombers over Sussex,* p 63, Midhurst: Middleton Press
[65] Goss C, op cit, Ch 6
[66] CMHQ Report 106
[67] Saunders A, (1990) *The Blitz – Then & Now,* p 215, London: Battle of Britain Prints International
[68] Goss C, op cit, Ch 7
[69] Number 6 Gun of E Troop, 53 Bty, 11 LAA Regt (RHQ 16 South Cliff Ave). In June 1943, 53 Bty HQ was at Folkington Manor, Nr Polegate, with E Troop at St Cyprian's Lodge, 65 Summerdown Rd. E Troop's Number 6 Gun was at MR593980, on the lower track 200m WSW of the reservoir.

Operation Jubilee

[70] Milton R & Callaghan R (2005), *The Redoubt Fortress and Martello Towers of Eastbourne.* Ch 4, Eastbourne: Eastbourne Local History Society

Listening to the enemy

[71] Gates R & Weicker, Col C J, *The Original Canadian Spies of the Airwaves.* Ottawa: Comms and Electronics, Dept National Defence, www.rcsigs.ca
[72] ibid
[73] ibid
[74] Corbett J, *Personal Recollections 99/4611,* London: IWM

Ubique

[75] Longstaff-Tyrrell P (1997) *Operation Cuckmere Haven,* Ch 18, Polegate: Gote House
[76] Kerry Col A J & McDill Maj W A (1966) *The History of the Corps of Royal Canadian Engineers – Vol 2.* Canada: Military Engineering Institute of Canada

Home on the range

[77] Donne J (1947) *Sussex County Magazine* Vol 21
[78] Surtees J (1997) *Beachy Head,* Ch 8, Seaford: S B Publications
[79] Huggett C (1995) *Drusillas Railway – 60 Years of Narrow Gauge.* Alfriston: Drusillas Zoo Park
[80] Donne J, op cit
[81] Goss C, op cit, Appendix 5, 6 & 8
[82] Dobinson C (2001) *AA Command.* London: Methuen

Thanks for the memory

[83] Smith, Lt L N, op cit

Index

Index

Index

The author

Michael Ockenden was born in Eastbourne in 1938 and became interested in history thanks to the inspiration of John Harrison, Senior History Master at Eastbourne Grammar School. After a year in the Merchant Navy as a Radio Officer, he served as an Air Electronics Officer in the Royal Air Force with 617 and 50 Squadrons, also qualifying as a Linguist. For 30 years he was Co-Principal of the English Centre in St Anne's Road. Apart from the Canadian Army in Britain, his historical interests include the raid by 617 Squadron on the Ruhr Dams, the development of television and the German home front. He has been a member of Eastbourne Local History Society since its inception in 1970.